Boulez on Conducting

BOULEZ
ON CONDUCTING

Conversations with Cécile Gilly

translated by Richard Stokes

faber and faber

First published in French in 2002
by Christian Bourgois éditeur
© by Christian Bourgois éditeur 2002
This translation first published in Great Britain in 2003
by Faber and Faber Limited
3 Queen Square London WC1N 3AU

Typeset by Faber and Faber Limited
Printed in England by Mackays of Chatham, plc

A CIP record for this book
is available from the British Library

ISBN 0-571-21967-5

2 4 6 8 10 9 7 5 3 1

Contents

Foreword

Pierre Boulez is known today throughout the world as one of the major composers of the twentieth century and as an orchestral conductor who has campaigned to give the music of his century its rightful place in the repertoire, and to redefine the art of conducting. He has also never ceased contributing to contemporary musical thought, or commenting on the artistic positions he has held and the concerts he has given.

For some time now, he has wanted to look back on his career as a conductor, and express his thoughts on the art of conducting. The conversations gathered here were originally recorded for France-Musiques and filmed by ARTE and they bear witness to, amongst other things, the creation of IRCAM, the founding of the Ensemble Intercontemporain and the setting up of the Cité de la Musique project, all of which were closely linked to his activity as a performer. Fiercely committed to his own times, he explains in this book the circumstances that led him to build a centre where scientists and musicians could speak the same language, and why it was necessary to found an ensemble of soloists dedicated to the repertoire of the twentieth century and the creation of new works. He also tells us why he has devoted so much time to conducting, sometimes at the risk of neglecting his activity as a composer.

But beyond all these issues, we learn what it is like to be a conductor. We discover how he analyses his own music or that of other composers, past and present, in order to decide on the most appropriate gesture with which to communicate to the audience his understanding of a work. These conversations also show us Boulez as a teacher, anxious to pass on, through stimulating masterclasses in France and the rest of the world, the fruits of his own unique experience, through which he has revolutionized not only musical language but also the art of conducting.

Boulez on Conducting is neither a book about musicology nor a theoretical treatise. It provides us with first-hand information that allows us to glimpse the man behind the composer and the conductor: a determined individual, capable of sudden outbursts and moments of great relaxation, always passionately concerned about the sound of his compositions and how that sound can be conveyed to an intelligent and sensitive audience through the art of conducting.

Jean-Jacques Nattiez
Paris, 2003

Translator's Note

I am grateful to the following friends and colleagues for answering individual queries: Susan Bradshaw, Dr Jacqueline Cockburn, Mark Elder, Virginie Guichard, Dr Jonathan Katz, Maurice Lynn, Belinda and Colin Matthews, Jane Pountney, Dr Sinan Carter Savaskan, Roger Vignoles and John Clifford Witney. Particular thanks are due to Julian Anderson for reading through the whole manuscript and making many valuable suggestions.

Musicians and other personalities appearing in the book are listed in the Index of names.

I

From Stage Music to the *Ring*

A flying start

CÉCILE GILLY: *Before discussing in detail the purely techni-*
cal questions concerning your double activity as conductor
and composer, I should like to know how you became an
orchestral conductor.

PIERRE BOULEZ: My beginnings were very modest. I had
absolutely no intention of becoming a conductor. Conducting simply entered my existence and then took over – sometimes, through my own fault, a little too much. No one is to
blame but myself. From 1946 to 1956, I worked for the
Renaud– Barrault organization, where I was in charge of
stage music. And so I began very unobtrusively to conduct
a band of some twelve or fifteen instruments. Initially, I was
extremely awkward. I can recall my first efforts in 1946 –
which were far from brilliant, even though the music,
God only knows, was of no great complexity. And then,
having learned to swim, I was thrown in at the deep end. In
1953, when I began conducting the Domaine Musicale
concerts, which featured the music of the Second Viennese
school and also the works of the youngest composers of
that time – Stockhausen, Berio, Nono, Pousseur and myself
– I very quickly found myself faced with a problem. Roger
Désormière, who was one of the few musicians capable of
conducting these concerts, had just suffered a heart attack
and was practically paralysed. Hermann Scherchen and
Hans Rosbaud were at that time approaching their sixties
and had many engagements, as did Ernest Bour, who conducted the concerts two or three times. And since the

Domaine Musicale's financial resources were very limited, I told myself that, being much less expensive, I would have a go myself. I was fortunate to be surrounded by musicians who loved playing contemporary music, and played it with me and for me with a lot of friendship and warmth. And so it came about that I conducted Stockhausen's *Kontrapunkte*, as well as pieces by Pousseur. Having finished *Le marteau sans maître*, I wanted Hans Rosbaud to come with his players from Baden-Baden and give the first performance of the work in Paris in 1956. Rosbaud was not available and so, with the concert already advertised, I found myself without a conductor. No conductor, and no players either. I decided to take my courage in both hands, and we began to rehearse. We were none of us especially skilled. In the end, we were pleased to get through the piece without a catastrophe. And little by little I discovered how to conduct an orchestra.

You then worked in Germany from 1958 to 1959.

I had the good fortune to be put in charge of the music department of the Südwestfunk of Baden-Baden, where I was entrusted with ever larger groups. I needed all my strength not to panic, because I was still not very accomplished. Previously, in 1957, I had conducted the first version of *Le visage nuptial* in Cologne. Then, with Maderna, Stockhausen and the orchestra of the West Deutscher Rundfunk, we gave the first performance of Stockhausen's *Gruppen*. It was through conducting works by the composers of my own generation that I really began. And, as is often the case, it was an exceptional event that caused me to take the plunge. In 1959 Hans Rosbaud fell ill and asked me to take his place in Aix-en-Provence and conduct . . . not Mozart, but a concert of contemporary music that was part of the festival. The programme consisted of Webern's *Six Pieces* Op. 6, three extracts from Berg's *Wozzeck*, a work by Hindemith composed in the twenties called *Philharmonisches Konzert*, and *Rimes*, a new work by Pousseur. I told myself: 'No matter how great the challenge, it must be done, and done well.' I had made it a point of honour to change nothing in the programme, which I had even learned by heart – an excellent discipline for a beginner. With Rosbaud still unwell, Heinrich Strobel, director of music at Radio Baden-Baden, asked me to replace him at the Donaueschingen Festival. I told him I felt incapable of doing so. He replied: 'That is the only way of saving the festival, you must come.' Rosbaud had rehearsed these two programmes for almost a fortnight with the orchestra, but he had been rushed to hospital again in Zurich and I could not even ask him for advice. And so I found myself in front of the orchestra, who were, it must be said, very kind. I took charge of the concert, which was very long, owing to the changes that had to be made to the stage. The last piece on the programme was Bartók's *Miraculous Mandarin*, which ends with the wild dance of the mandarin. I recall that the wait caused by regrouping the orchestra on stage was enormously long; I had to work hard to control my stage fright – for although Rosbaud had prepared the orchestra, it was for me a 'première'. In the end, it did not go too badly, since I thought the best way of coping was to proceed with 'ferocity', whatever the cost, without fear and without worrying about criticism! I really don't know about the quality of the concert, or even whether it has been preserved somewhere in the archives, but I do remember that both the festival audience and the organizers were overwhelmed by the explosive entrance of the orchestra. And so my career got off to a flying start.

What, him! Conduct *Parsifal*!

Several German radio orchestras had asked me to conduct for them. I had also stood in for Rosbaud at the Concertgebouw in Amsterdam, which led to contacts in America, particularly Cleveland, thanks to Georg Szell. One thing then led to another: I was invited by William Glock, the Controller of Music at the BBC, to conduct the BBC Symphony Orchestra. The career of an orchestral conductor took me by surprise.

At this point in your career, you were only conducting twentieth-century works.

Exclusively, and only recently composed works at that. At the Concertgebouw, however, I had to learn the Classical repertoire. One of my first concerts included a symphony by Haydn. If you conduct the modern repertoire, it is automatically assumed that you know nothing at all about any other period of music. In 1966, when I conducted *Parsifal* at Bayreuth, people exclaimed: 'What, him! Conduct *Parsifal*!' It seemed to them as incongruous as if I had been put in charge of building a museum! This extremely blinkered view of human knowledge is grotesque and absurd, quite apart from the fact that it reveals the arrogance of people for whom I have very little respect, who consider themselves the guardians of our culture and yet have absolutely no idea of modern music.

Can you remember your first operatic experience?

You always remember the first time you conduct an opera. In my case, it was Berg's *Wozzeck*, not one of the easiest works to conduct, in Jean-Louis Barrault's 1963 production in Paris. I knew the work well, having analysed it during a music congress in Basle, and I knew it well from a recording by Dimitri Mitropoulos with the New York Philharmonic Orchestra. Although I was more familiar with this score than that of any other opera, I still asked Georges Auric, the Director of the Opéra, for thirty rehearsals for the fifteen scenes of *Wozzeck*, and I therefore had time to prepare the work properly. In any case, I had nothing to lose, even though the orchestra had never played the work nor any of that repertoire. I also knew the director very well – Jean-Louis Barrault, with whom I had worked between 1946 and 1956. The advantages, therefore, were all on my side. The designer was André Masson and the cast was German, since I very much wanted to perform *Wozzeck* in the original language. Operas at that time were often sung in French translation. I could remember a performance of *Wozzeck* in German in Paris some time in 1952, with Karl Böhm conducting the Vienna State Opera, and I had heard a radio performance by the Orchestre Nationale in French translation. Performing the work in French poses many problems, particularly in the fourth scene of the third act, where Wozzeck, having killed Marie, sings the crucial phrase 'le couteau', referring to the knife that he has lost in the water and is now desperate to find. In German, he sings 'das Messer', on a rising and descending third, which corresponds exactly to the tonic stress of the German language; in French, however, the accent falls on the 'cou' of 'le *cou*teau', which is completely wrong!

That's why in 1963 I was so keen to have a German cast – which posed absolutely no problems for Jean-Louis Barrault, who rehearsed the singers. Despite my anxiety, I have a very positive memory of the occasion, and I have to say that I was greatly helped by ten years' experience working with Jean-Louis Barrault on theatrical projects. Although much of this music was not very complex, I had conducted Milhaud's *Christophe Colomb*; and working with actors had taught me how to adapt the tempo of an orchestra to the pace of the words. Though my experience was very limited, it certainly helped me to conduct *Wozzeck*.

Wozzeck paved the way for Bayreuth. In the spring of 1966, I conducted it in Wieland Wagner's production at the Frankfurt Opera, and in the summer of the same year I conducted *Parsifal* at Bayreuth. I had got to know Wieland at a time when I had no fixed engagements with any orchestra. I was as free as air. That is why we were able to plan productions of *Don Giovanni*, *Elektra*, *Lulu*, *Boris Godunov*, *Tristan und Isolde* and *Pelléas et Mélisande*. I would willingly have hitched, if not my entire fate, then at least a part of it, to someone like him, for such discussions about music and productions were thrilling. When Wieland Wagner died prematurely in November 1966, all these projects fell through, except *Tristan und Isolde*, which I conducted in his production at the Osaka Festival in 1967, and *Pelléas*, on which we were to have collaborated – in both these cases, the contracts had already been signed. I conducted *Pelléas* in 1969 in Josef Svoboda's production at Covent Garden, and recorded it in the wake of those performances. I seem to remember that the last Covent Garden production of the opera had been given by Désormière before an invited audience and with the cast of the 1940s, including Irène Joachim and Jacques Jansen. I then revived *Pelléas* two years later at Covent Garden, in 1971.

After the death of Wieland, I waited ten years before working again with such stimulating and committed opera directors – namely Patrice Chéreau and Peter Stein. So it came about that, through Daniel Barenboim, I conducted *Pelléas* for a second time, on this occasion in Cardiff. Barenboim was in charge of the Opéra Bastille, and for three or four years we had been working together on projects in an attempt to create a true partnership between conductor and director. I was to conduct *Pelléas* and *Moses and Aaron* in Peter Stein's productions of these works. Following Barenboim's dismissal, *Pelléas* was first performed at Cardiff, then at the Châtelet in Paris. As had been the case with Wieland Wagner, I was now working with a great director of my own choice. I then conducted Peter Stein's production of Schoenberg's *Moses and Aaron* in Amsterdam and Salzburg.

Curiously enough, Stein did not initially wish to direct *Pelléas*. I had met him to discuss the centenary *Ring* at Bayreuth. I had contacted him before Patrice Chéreau quite simply because I did not know the situation in France; at that time I wasn't living in Paris. But things did not work out with him. I conducted Chéreau's *Ring* from 1976 to 1980, and also his production of Berg's *Lulu* at the Paris Opéra, in the three-act version completed by Friedrich Cerha. I met Peter Stein again later, and we spoke once more about *Pelléas* and *Moses and Aaron*. He was very much for *Moses and Aaron*, but less convinced by *Pelléas*, perhaps because, from the outside, French music still had the reputation of being 'perfumed'. But Debussy is something quite different, and he finally agreed to direct *Pelléas*.

Did you ever meet other musicians who were both composers and conductors? I'm thinking, for example, of Bruno Maderna and Michael Gielen.

Not very often, to be honest. There were several occasions, of course, when we saw each other conduct. I'm thinking above all of Maderna in Darmstadt; we were sometimes confronted by scores that were absolutely mad. It was the era of aleatoric music, and the scores sometimes looked like a game of Monopoly. It was none the less interesting for each of us to see how the other set about the task. We both ended up learning a good deal from these experiences. Even if musically they were not very fruitful, they forced us to be inventive and imaginative from the point of view of conducting. I met Gielen a little later. We belong to the same generation, and we both underwent a certain number of similar experiences. He is someone that you can trust implicitly to conduct contemporary music with expertise and intelligence. At Strasburg or Baden-Baden I also met Ernest Bour, someone who is unfortunately too little known in France and who has made an enormous contribution to contemporary music. His way of conducting, based on a most detailed knowledge of the score, acquired a high degree of precision; he was totally committed to modern music. The Donaueschingen Festival owes him – and his predecessor, Hans Rosbaud – an enormous debt.

A winter in Strasburg

Was your own style influenced by your experience with the more Classical repertoire? I'm thinking of Mahler, Wagner and Berg.

Anyone who conducts Mahler's symphonies, as I did in London and New York, and Wagner's *Ring* is bound to be immersed in a different musical dimension. I was well aware of this dimension, but it has to be said that little attention was paid in my musical education to these composers, although Messiaen had a great affection for Wagner. And Messiaen, at this period, was sailing completely against the wind. Ever since certain criticisms were raised by Debussy and Stravinsky, to mention but two of the most eminent names, Wagner was considered to be the acme of an insufferable and 'outmoded' Germanness . . . As for Mahler, he was practically never played in France. And I did not actually discover him for myself until 1958, when I started living in Germany. All I can remember from before that is a performance of the Fourth Symphony conducted by Paul Kletzki, and *Das Lied von der Erde* conducted by Bruno Walter – absolutely nothing else.

Do you think that it is useful for a composer to be a conductor? Or vice versa?

The only times when it is useful and profitable for a conductor to know something of composition are when he is confronted by a complex score. I'm thinking of Berg's

Three Pieces Op.6, where it's necessary to make clear an extremely dense musical texture. Analysis helps you then to distinguish the hierarchies and the levels, and to organize the progression of the piece. In the past, even if they weren't top-flight composers, great orchestral conductors such as Furtwängler and Klemperer had first-hand experience of composition – as did Hans von Bülow in the nineteenth century. It is certainly no disadvantage to have studied and practised composition – on the contrary. None the less, there are musicians who have a more intuitive knowledge of things, and they should not for that reason be dismissed. Instrumentalists, in particular, can deepen this intuitive knowledge enormously merely by playing and glancing through the scores. Such a knowledge is just as valid as any other, once it totally absorbs the work. As for those composers who wish at all costs to conduct, I think that it's impossible to force one's talent. But to have to grapple with the art of conducting one's own works, and with small forces, can only be beneficial if the composer feels both the need and the wish to do so; that can teach him much more swiftly and effectively about the validity of his own speculations than any advice, however well intentioned. Unfortunately, the life of a professional musician hardly lends itself to this sort of apprenticeship.

That has not been so in your case . . .

No. But I recall the impact that Roger Désormière first made on me; he embodied for my generation the sort of conductor who was interested in contemporary music, including the most adventurous and recent repertoire. He was also extremely sympathetic; I had got to know him well personally because during the winter of 1949 I found myself alone in Strasburg playing the ondes martenot in an opera by Marcel Delannoy.

That hardly sounds like you . . .

No, not exactly! But Marcel Delannoy arrived at that time to rehearse and conduct Stravinsky's *The Nightingale*, which formed part of a programme from which I can remember nothing else. I attended every single rehearsal, and I can still remember the way he 'dissected' this score which was completely unknown to me. Afterwards, he took me out to dinner and we talked for a long time about conducting technique and interpretation. Then I saw him rehearse *Les noces* in Paris. It was he who taught me how to master the unequal stress patterns on which Stravinsky's metre is based, and what exercises I should practise in order to acquire the necessary reflexes for conducting this sort of rhythmic music.

'Hello, Otto Klemperer speaking'

You were also in touch with other great conductors at this period, notably Otto Klemperer, who was very interested in contemporary music, even if he didn't conduct it himself.

When I first met him, he was no longer conducting contemporary music, although he had often done so in the past when working at the Kroll Opera in Berlin between the wars. Like the Vienna State Opera, this was an adventurous opera house where scandals were not only created by premières of new works but also by innovative productions of, say, Beethoven and Wagner within the repertoire. These modern productions were deemed to be extremely provocative. The Kroll Opera did much for the contemporary music of that period and Klemperer himself was personally involved, conducting Schoenberg, Stravinsky and Hindemith. It is, of course, the eighty-year-old Klemperer whom one remembers most, the admired interpreter of Beethoven, Brahms, Bruckner and Mahler, but the years he spent in Berlin should not be forgotten. He seldom came to conduct in Paris, but he was frequently in London, where he was greatly loved – and it was there that I first met him. One morning, I received a phone call and heard the unmistakably characteristic voice which orchestral musicians often imitated: 'Hello, Otto Klemperer speaking.' I thought at first it was a joke – but not a bit of it: it was him, asking me if he could attend the rehearsals of the concert which was to include *Le soleil des eaux*. He came and attended the rehearsals from beginning to end; the programme, by the way, also contained Bartók's Second Piano Concerto with Geza Anda as soloist. He also turned up much later, when I was conducting *Parsifal* in Bayreuth. The ideological content of this work irritated him beyond measure. He asked me: 'How can you put up with this pseudo-religious mess?' I replied that I was less concerned with this side of the work – which was, anyway, debatable – than with the exceptional musical quality of the score. After the performance, we talked about the violent controversies, begun by Nietzsche, that stem from this type of transfiguration of the Wagnerian self through religious ceremony. It was a passionate discussion, for Klemperer as a man was extraordinarily pugnacious.

Were you aware that he also composed?

Of course!

Did you know his works?

I got to know them a long time after I first met him.

Very few conductors were as frank and open as Désormière and Klemperer.

Very few. But even today, you can count the great musical directors on the fingers of one hand. They are what we lack most, and there are many reasons for this: firstly, today's conductors lack culture. They are not familiar with the whole range of music, and they restrict themselves to a limited repertoire. Secondly, they lack flair. They only rarely seem to have a sense of discovery, only rarely have an intuition of what might become really valuable. Thirdly, they do not know how to run an institution in an artistic way: namely, without bludgeoning the listener, to make him aware of the inevitable shift in language and sensibility. Very few music directors have this vision of their profession. I would not say that such a vision is easily acquired, but I maintain that it is indispensable if one wishes to assume these responsibilities vis-à-vis oneself and others.

The tempi in *Parsifal*

It was Wieland Wagner who invited you to conduct Parsifal
*at Bayreuth, following the sudden death of Hans Knapperts-
busch. Until then, there had never been a single mention of
the composer in your writings; it was the first time that you
had been confronted with a work by Richard Wagner.*

It was also the first time that I had conducted at Bayreuth.
Before then, I only knew two operas by Wagner: *Tristan und
Isolde* and *Die Meistersinger*, certain passages of which had
been analysed by Messiaen in the classes I attended at the
Paris Conservatoire. And *Die Meistersinger* had been one of
the first operas I saw as a student in Lyon in 1942 or the
spring of 1943; I had also seen *Boris Godunov*. Both works
were conducted by André Cluytens, and both remain firm
favourites of mine. Oddly enough, Cluytens was supposed to
have replaced Knappertsbusch, who was too ill to conduct at
Bayreuth; but he then fell ill himself. Was this fate, I wonder?
I'm not sure whether Wieland Wagner would have entrusted
me with *Parsifal* if Cluytens had not fallen ill. He knew me as
a conductor, because I had performed *Wozzeck* at the Paris
Opéra, and also through Karl-Amadeus Hartmann, who
organized the Musica Viva concerts in Munich, where I had
conducted a number of works by Debussy. Hartmann had
said to Wieland: 'If you are looking for a conductor for *Parsifal*, he is your man.' That's how the connection with
Bayreuth came about.

How were you received at the Festspielhaus?

When I arrived, I was astonished at how well things went. We rehearsed the singers in a wooden hut that was also a restaurant – such double functions are not uncommon in Bayreuth. Rehearsals are still held in this same restaurant today – it was built to last, and is now much better equipped than in 1966. Everything went really well. It has to be said that *Parsifal* is probably one of the easiest of Wagner's operas to conduct. Those great expanses of time, such as the chorus scenes of Acts 1 and 3 – everything, in other words, that relates to ceremony – are moments in which one can feel fairly quickly at ease. But there are, of course, more difficult scenes of greater contrast, notably in Act 2, where the sense of drama is heightened. The tempi in general are rather slow or moderate; in the long term, this allows you time to settle. Compared with *Wozzeck*, the first opera I conducted, conducting technique did not seem to me to be the problem. Although interpretation is clearly not just a problem of technique, the performance is bound to gain a greater sense of freedom if the conductor is not hampered by a lack of technique.

Apropos tempi, why do interpretations of this work vary so much? How do you find the right tempo?

The most celebrated example is Toscanini, normally known for his excessively fast tempi. In this work, he broke all records for slowness – which can be explained in the first place by the feeling that in *Parsifal* one is tackling with respect and devotion a work that is essentially religious. The ceremonial and ritual aspects are evident most of all in Acts 1 and 3; the second act has a highly erotic charge, and calls for agitation and trance-like ecstasy. The very term 'religious' suggests solemnity, and in the conducting tradition solemnity is normally expressed by means of a slow beat. That, to me, is a mistake: although *feierlich* translates as 'solemn', that does not necessarily imply a 'slow' tempo; solemnity in happiness can even be construed as a lively tempo, without resorting to hysteria. And then there is the 'Bayreuth' phenomenon, less pronounced now, but enormously influential in the past. I spoke to Wieland Wagner about it and he told me an anecdote which must have come from his family – that Wagner was extremely annoyed at the exaggeratedly slow tempi adopted during rehearsals. Apparently he often summoned Hermann Levi, the conductor entrusted with the first performance, and pleaded: 'Faster, faster, don't drag.' One can see that *Parsifal*, from the very beginning, was plagued by slow tempi.

It's also perhaps something to do with the hugely imposing choral sound.

I think it has more to do with the way the stage is organized. At the end of the third act, for example, the choirs are placed on three levels, ranging from the stage to the cupola. Wagner had taken Siena Cathedral as his model, and the time that the sound needs to travel means that each group waits for the others in order to be able to hear – slowness imposes itself inexorably. You need to ignore the inevitable acoustic delay that the dispersed choirs have to cope with. Another difficulty has to do with the acoustic of that famous orchestra pit which is both covered and sloping down. The acoustic, heard from the auditorium, is a pure miracle, but initially it's somewhat difficult to get used to. You often have the impression that the orchestra is playing too loudly for the singers, who seem far distant, especially when they are at the back of the stage. The conductor is situated 'in' the sound of the orchestra, while the voices of the singers pass over you directly into the auditorium. This tempts you to slow down, since hearing is tantamount to waiting, and that is precisely what you must not do.

This difference in tempi is therefore not simply a question of how you perceive the work, but is partly due to the acoustics . . .

The two are certainly not mutually exclusive. Religious feeling and acoustics – an unlikely marriage . . .

Programme planning at the BBC

After Cleveland, where you were invited by Georg Szell, you came to the BBC in 1971.

I was the Principal Conductor of the BBC Symphony Orchestra, the equivalent of Music Director in America. My arrival at the BBC had been planned over a long period. At the invitation of William Glock, I had regularly conducted this orchestra since 1964. Glock has been very important in my life: he had a vivid imagination, great inventiveness and absolutely reliable taste. He had a most thorough knowledge of both the Classical and the Romantic repertoires, but he was also passionately interested in contemporary music, for which he worked unrelentingly and showed great judgement. His arrival as Controller of Music had an enormous influence on the development of the BBC – not just the repertoire of the orchestra but also its quality. He engaged me regularly from 1964 to 1967, but less frequently as the years went by. Being involved more regularly and continuously at the BBC is due as much to chance as conscious decision. Wieland Wagner, with whom, as I've said, I had planned a number of operatic projects, died in 1966, and because of this everything now fell through. And anyway, I was interested at least as much in his exceptional personality as in the repertoire that we had chosen.

A year later, in 1967, Jean Vilar asked me to help get the Palais Garnier back into shape, and work on this project with Maurice Béjart. The events of 1968 intervened, and once again everything foundered. The Vilar report languished at the bottom of some drawer in the Ministry of Culture. It was then that William Glock came to find me in Holland, where I was giving a series of concerts, and invited me to succeed Colin Davis, who had been appointed Musical Director at Covent Garden. I accepted immediately in principle, and postponed discussions on the practical details of how we would work together. Glock taught me many things, in particular how to plan programmes and how to organize a season; our two approaches, mine more speculative, his more pragmatic, blended very well. In spring 1969 I signed the contract.

What were your artistic aims at that time? What sort of programmes did you wish to conduct?

I conducted everything. Absolutely everything; the orchestra needed to have a vast repertoire and had to play music from every period. It was not yet the norm to specialize in a restricted repertoire, as it is today. The symphonic repertoire seemed to begin with Haydn, and even he was not played much! There was little interest in baroque music, but I conducted it none the less.

I created three types of concerts. Those at the Festival Hall often contained a mixture of Classical and contemporary works. We also programmed, amongst other things, Stravinsky and Schoenberg festivals, as well as a fair number of world premières. A second type of concert tended to concentrate on chamber music: the orchestra was divided into two ensembles, enabling us to play a more extensive repertoire. I was thus able to conduct works that were very little known, such as Schubert's *Lazarus* or Schumann's *Der Rose Pilgerfahrt* – reading through the scores of these works had held my interest. We sometimes managed to include several contemporary works, but in general this series was devoted to works of the past which were either unusual or rarely performed. These concerts took place at St John's Smith Square, near Westminster, one of those eighteenth-century churches that are fairly common in London; the acoustics are unfortunately too resonant for contemporary music, and even for music of earlier periods. Since the area around St John's was almost entirely given over to businesses, we gave our concerts in the early evening, or sometimes at lunch-time, when people could leave their offices for a while.

Finally, there were those concerts entirely devoted to contemporary music. We gave first performances of composers of all nationalities, which took place at the Round House. These concerts were more informal and included a presentation of the work by the composer, if he happened to be in London, and a discussion with the audience at the end. These could sometimes be rather chaotic, as the contributions from members of the audience were not always to the point.

Were these concerts well attended?

Absolutely: we attracted very loyal audiences. The orchestra willingly subjected itself to these experiments, which were inevitably not always fruitful; but experimentation is much easier with limited forces . . .

New York's 'Zigzag' concerts

When you arrived in New York a little later in your career, things were rather different.

Yes, because the system was different. At the BBC, we didn't depend directly on the box office – which left us considerable room for manœuvre. When it transpired that five or six days of rehearsal were indispensable for a large-scale project, we could organize things without abusing this privilege. A broadcasting corporation subsidized by the state is not obliged to give four concerts a week with an identical programme, simply to fill the coffers. American orchestras are totally dependent on private donations and box-office takings. The survival of such institutions is based on a system of season-ticket subscriptions which unfortunately has to be inflexible. The general pattern is to have four rehearsals and four concerts a week – eight sessions in all. The arrangement is not open to discussion – to change it would need special authorization and extra financial backing.

Were you appointed because of your reputation as a composer–conductor?

The panel knew in advance what it had to do. I wasn't totally unknown in New York; they knew what I had achieved in London, and also that I had spent two seasons with the Cleveland Orchestra. The three weeks of concerts I had conducted in New York during the spring of 1969 were all representative of the sort of music I liked to programme; it has always been my aim to pay equal attention to both the twentieth century and the standard repertoire. All went well during these three weeks, and to my great surprise I was asked to become the Musical Director of the orchestra. By a funny coincidence, I was offered the post on 1 April!

I have to admit that, when I first took over, subscriptions declined because the repertoire was judged to be too adventurous; but numbers increased with a different type of audience who were more inquiring and more ready to listen to music of their own time. I would quite often include a twentieth-century 'classic' in a programme, and I was also keen to première several new works per season.

Did you mostly conduct works by American composers?

I conducted or programmed composers from all countries and from different backgrounds, despite the fact that I had a reputation for excluding and condemning certain music. I have always been in favour of multinational programmes, and though I have concentrated on local or national composers, this was never to the exclusion of other music. If one specializes too narrowly, one fails to do justice to the sort of music one wishes to promote; that very music even loses its credibility.

There were also concerts devoted to contemporary music.

Yes, and they took place downtown, where a fair number of intellectuals, artists and students live. As in London, I tried to organize concerts for a more adventurous sort of audience; there were only about half a dozen a year, and the players could choose whether they wished to participate or not. I asked them whether they were interested in this sort of approach, and those who decided to take part in the concerts did so with conviction.

Did you continue in New York with the same sort of programme planning that you had experimented with in London?

Yes. Each season, I introduced one or two themes which did not exactly dominate the planning but provided 'chapter headings'. I concentrated on the works of Liszt, for example: without wishing to mount an exhaustive retrospective, we revived certain works that were rarely played, and we performed them alongside Liszt's more popular pieces. To select these works, I sometimes needed to consult scores in the music library at the Lincoln Center in New York – I was very well received there, and was one of the few conductors to consult their enormous catalogue.

I also programmed a number of works by Haydn, not just the symphonies but extracts from the operas or masses which were at that time very seldom played. And I created the equivalent of the famous Proms. We called these 'Rug Concerts', because we took out all the seats and the orchestra played in the middle of the auditorium, surrounded by the audience. I divided the orchestra into two or three different formations to play, for example, the early symphonies of Mendelssohn, Mozart and Haydn. That also enabled us to tackle Schoenberg's *Serenade*, or the *Aventures* or *Nouvelles aventures* by Ligeti. This kind of arrangement also proved to be very interesting for the players, not just because of the different repertoire, but because it brought out their individual qualities in a small ensemble; the string players in particular felt freed from the usual orchestral throng. I had to be careful to distribute everything fairly, for the musicians who had been forgotten or assigned to pieces they were not at home with were not slow to criticize.

I also organized what I called mini-festivals: the first was built around Schubert, but later in 1974 there was one on Charles Ives, to celebrate the centenary of his birth. I devised a programme around Ives consisting mostly of American music from the years between 1925 and 1930, a very active period for avant-garde music, before the situation deteriorated badly with the recession and the Depression. We were thus able to give extremely varied concerts. I also programmed Ravel's highly Classical *Sonata for violin and cello* as well as Ives's *Fourth Symphony*, a turbulent piece for large orchestra. I liked these 'Zigzag' programmes, and the way they moved unexpectedly and abruptly from a flute concerto by Mozart to Ligeti's *Aventures* and *Nouvelles aventures*, juxtaposing different eras and styles.

An eventful return to Bayreuth

Your next major project was to mount a production of Wagner's Ring *at Bayreuth with Patrice Chéreau. Was this a long-standing project?*

Yes. I had heard the *Ring* during my first visit to Bayreuth in 1966, conducted by Karl Böhm in the production by Wieland Wagner. Having seen the work from the auditorium, I later attended a performance in the pit, to watch Böhm conduct.

It is well known that the audience gave you a rather hostile reception; but so, too, during rehearsals, did the singers and the orchestra, who were not used to your concept of the work.

As far as the singers are concerned, it's certainly true that some of them were not especially kind; one of them was, in fact, particularly hostile. When one encounters singers who have sung their role for many years, it is sometimes necessary to jolt them out of their routine. When you ask things of them that they do not agree with, their first reaction is to think that you are ignorant. Although it is not possible to know everything, this does not necessarily mean that one is an ignoramus.

My concern was, above all, to look for contrasts, while also maintaining the indispensable unity of the work. There were some singers who understood this unreservedly, but there were others who certainly did not. As the years went by, the ideal cast was chosen, and they happily began to understand what I had in mind.

What style of performance was prevalent when you arrived?

The performances, in my view, lacked nuance and finesse. The text was 'barked' and thus erased the dynamic and rhythmic precision by which Wagner set such store. I asked for nothing more than that. Routine had gradually distorted things that had been learned, standards were no longer respected, had been vulgarized without reference to the original text.

Did the orchestra display the same faults?

In matters of precision and detail, I clashed with certain members of the orchestra who were convinced that expression was not possible without excess. It seems wrong to me systematically to equate expressiveness with dynamics: to play each crescendo as loudly as possible does not increase the expressive power of the music but literally clubs it senseless and annihilates it through overemphasis.

The transparent texture of Wagner's orchestra is for me just as essential as the huge blocks of sound that the composer also employs and which are not the most important aspect of his style. Justice must be done to the meticulous detail of his scores. The great difficulty is to reconcile, if I can put it like this, the specific detail with the overall shape.

Nor do I like imprecise playing. It's true that the strings at the very end of *Die Walküre* can only with difficulty play the arpeggios as written by Wagner with utterly sure intonation and at the correct speed. The same problem can be found in the 'Daybreak' movement of Ravel's *Daphnis et Chloé*. These arpeggios, however, must be sufficiently close to the actual intervals and must also be – and this is perfectly possible – rhythmically absolutely accurate. What the audience might perceive as 'transparent texture' stems more from accurate intonation than mere quality of sound. I attempted to achieve this goal, but not necessarily within the first year.

When you arrived at Bayreuth, did you have the impression that, as a conductor, you were completely revolutionizing the Ring?

Absolutely not, and neither was it my intention. When I read a score, there are various levels of sound that I wish to hear, and not just an indistinct mass; I try simultaneously to achieve an overall sound and to superimpose several distinct layers. To hear a score is, for me, to 'read' it: the ear must be faithful to the eye, the real sound must overlap as exactly as possible with the imagined sound. The great difficulty with Wagner is not only to attend to the detail of each moment but also at the same time to maintain the general line, and maintain it with confidence and determination, especially in the longest scenes.

I certainly didn't manage that within the first year, because it's only through habit that you can really master everything. Until you are confronted by the actual staging, you think in a much more intellectual way, without any spontaneity. What I achieved in the first year, as far as I can now judge, was bound to be partly artificial, because I was too much taken up with reflection: I was probably much more concerned with myself than with others. That said, I didn't encounter hostility because of any mistakes I made.

It's true that I stumbled on occasions, but only rarely, and that is not what should be remembered after so many hours of music.

My real problem had to do with questions of balance, transparency of texture and dynamic shading – things that I consider essential – without sacrificing, through excessive control, the expressive power of the music which lives through these things. If the orchestra forces, the singers will also force and the music will lack expression, become monotonous and lose all ability to render nuance. I was also concerned that the theatre should exist as a theatre and not merely a supporting adjunct to the music.

Didn't the fabled acoustic help you?

That's a question of psychology. The orchestral players cannot be seen; they feel that they are not seen, and think subconsciously that they cannot be heard – which encourages them to force. Imagine that you are at the very back of this pit, which is very deep. You will very likely feel you have to play loudly in order to balance what can be seen – in other words, the singers on stage – which is a mistake: the acoustics at Bayreuth are so good that if the orchestra plays *mezzo forte*, you will hear a *mezzo forte*, and if it plays *fortissimo*, you will hear a *fortissimo*.

In fact, you had a more radical vision of the score by virtue of being a composer, since you are used to writing dynamic nuances into your own scores. And this insistence of yours on accurate dynamics was certainly one of the reasons for the disputes you had with the players.

Probably, but it wasn't the only reason; communication

difficulties reached such a pitch that I began to ask myself: 'Do I really know how to conduct?' I remember that after the last performance of the *Ring* in 1976, I returned to London to conduct Bartók's *Bluebeard's Castle*. And I told myself: 'Yes, I still know how to conduct. The problems in Bayreuth were not all my fault!' When you have misgivings, you suppose that you lack some essential quality to achieve everything you want. I had already conducted *Wozzeck*, *Pelléas et Mélisande* and *Parsifal*; but with the *Ring*, things took a different turn. As the years passed, everything gradually improved; and in the end, I think the result was convincing enough.

There are works that you have never conducted but would have liked to tackle. I'm thinking of the project you had with Mozart, and also Mussorgsky, whom you often quote and whose works you have never played.

Never, that is true. I would have loved to conduct *Boris*. But as always, circumstances intervened: Wieland Wagner died, and I turned to the symphonic repertoire.

Is it not true to say that the repertoire you choose as conductor and musical director reflects your own preoccupations as a composer? That is to say, you choose certain composers who, like you, though in a different era, looked into the problems of renewing musical language?

Certainly. As a musical director, you have the advantage of being able to entrust pieces which you do not particularly wish to conduct to guest conductors who are happy to oblige because they love these works. I have therefore never been keen to conduct Prokofiev or Hindemith.

And you have never conducted Verdi either?

It's not the sort of music with which I feel in tune. The only work of his that I might have chosen is the *Quattro pezzi sacri*. Among the late works, if I had to choose between *Otello* and *Falstaff*, I would go for *Falstaff*. But if I were offered a different sort of choice, it would be *Die Meistersinger* and not *Falstaff*. We all have our little foibles.

II

A Look at Some Great Composer–Conductors

Berlioz and Wagner:
the birth of modern conducting

You have conducted the works of Berlioz and Wagner, the first composer–conductors to theorize in their writings about conducting an orchestra. Can we imagine them as conductors today, and do you think that their scores reveal the fact that they were conductors?

Their attitude vis-à-vis Beethoven was highly significant, because they both worked on him as apprentice conductors. In London, for example, they were both engaged for virtually the same repertoire. Contemporary newspaper reviews describe the manner in which Wagner and Berlioz conducted – and from them one can imagine that Berlioz conducted in a more precise, more delineated, more nervous way than Wagner, whose tempi were certainly more flexible and varied and whose sonority was more blended. This can also be found in their compositions. Take the *Symphonie fantastique*, the first great work by Berlioz, or the later *Roméo et Juliette* – in both pieces you will find a sort of rhythmic nervousness that requires a precision which was exceptional for the period. The 'Queen Mab' scherzo still remains one of the most difficult works to play with precision, even today.

Because of its rhythmic difficulty?

Because of the rapid and precise rhythms, the staccatos which must be even and regular in all registers, because of the isolated notes that occur right at the end of the bar, on the third quaver . . . All of which must fall into place with absolutely perfect precision. This style shows that Berlioz was extremely demanding with regard to rhythmic drive. Today, however, one can no longer recreate notions of ensemble, the balancing of chords, questions of intonation. Wagner's idea of rhythm, one imagines, was more supple. His writings on conducting reveal some very interesting thoughts. When he conducted what we call the 'classics' – Beethoven, in particular, who was his favourite composer – Wagner clashed with the conventions of his time. The critic Hanslick, who was a staunch supporter of a certain Classical tradition and a sworn enemy of Wagner, denounced in a most virulent way Wagner's habit of varying the tempo – claiming that it undermined the internal coherence of a work: since musical ideas were linked to a general tempo, such a procedure made the work chaotic. Wagner's writings, however, recommend that the tempo should be varied. He states that each musical idea must have its own rhythmic profile, its own impetus, its own tempo – and he gives several precise examples. It seems likely, in fact, that his essential concept was that of a progressive tempo – such as can be found in his own music. He applied this concept to the music of Beethoven, because he was also thinking of the genesis of his own music and of the way in which he wished it to be played. Wagner, incidentally, never showed any hostility towards Berlioz in this matter, whereas he harboured a deep and virulent hostility towards Mendelssohn, not just because of his anti-Semitism – a most disagreeable aspect of his personality – but because he considered that Mendelssohn lacked this flexibility of tempo, that everything was contained within the strait-jacket of an excessively rigid interpretation.

We are concerned here with the evolution of musical language. What Wagner calls the 'art of transition': the attempt to vary tempo according to the way in which the vocal or instrumental expression changes. Is this what he was referring to?

For Wagner, all music was, in effect, dramatic, especially the symphonies of Beethoven. And he was right, if you compare them with the symphonies of Mozart or Haydn. When you read Cosima's journal, which includes Wagner's informal comments on Beethoven, it is clear that he took the symphonies to be dramatic models. The prototype was, of course, the Ninth Symphony, in particular the 'choral' last movement with not only its vocal but its instrumental recitatives. It is impossible to conduct these recitatives in a rigid manner: they require a sort of declamation. I am convinced that Wagner, too, considered music a sort of declamation – not necessarily a verbal declamation, but a phrasing which reveals the dramatic content of the music.

Looking at the scores of Berlioz and Wagner, one is astonished by their precision, especially where dynamics or tempi are concerned. They even go so far as to plan how the chorus and orchestra should be placed on stage. What do you, as a conductor, think of this?

Both men were realists who, at their time, were concerned with the conditions in which their works were performed – something which was new; previously, musicians more or less put up with existing conditions. But with Berlioz and Wagner, great attention was paid to the staging and the whole theatrical set-up. *Lélio*, the continuation of the *Symphonie fantastique*, is a melodrama involving an actor in which the orchestra remains concealed until the final movement. The work concerns the autobiographical musings of a composer; to emphasize these musings, he imagines the orchestra to be invisible – something that Stockhausen also did in *Trans*. It's a curious fact that Berlioz's theatrical imagination is much stronger in his symphonic music than in his works for the theatre. There are enormous differences between Berlioz and Wagner, but both of them stem from the same roots: Beethoven, Gluck and Mozart, almost in that order, except that Mozart was probably much more important for Wagner than he was for Berlioz. The more Wagner develops, the more he owes to others – for example, Beethoven in the last quartets. His music undergoes a radical evolution of language, whereas his theatrical ideas hardly develop. They were virtually decided on as early as *Der fliegende Holländer* and *Tannhäuser*, although they saw a refinement in the *Ring*, which is dramatically infinitely more interesting. All his operas belong to the early days of Romanticism, Gothic Romanticism, whereas Berlioz is attracted by neo-Classical antiquity.

In *Les Troyens*, Berlioz takes Gluck as his model, with all the stylistic consequences which that implied. There is a divergence of point of view, therefore, which has led to irreconcilable differences between them as regards conducting. Whereas Wagner's music, given the suppleness of his forms and transitions, becomes more and more characterized by fluidity, flexibility and changing tempi, Berlioz's works become more and more set in isolated categories, which implies a specific tempo for a piece, an aria, an ensemble – except in recitatives, where there is a greater freedom. But Berlioz, unlike Wagner, did not invest the musical flow itself with this freedom. The difficulty with

Wagner is that the variations of tempi seemed so necessary, so natural to him, that he did not often indicate them in detail in the score. Sometimes there are more precise indications in those scores that were printed in Germany, prepared by his assistant and by artists who attended rehearsals in Wagner's own time. Many of these directions are negative in tone, like 'do not hurry' – which proves above all that these assistants were pointing out the shortcomings of the performers; and since the composer corrected these deficiencies, the observations on interpretation are inevitably more often negative than positive. With Berlioz, one has no reference point, apart from some personal remarks that are generally sarcastic, because he was infinitely more isolated than Wagner, isolated as a person and isolated in Paris, a city that was fundamentally hostile towards him, whereas Wagner, especially from 1870 onwards, was surrounded by admirers.

If one considers Berlioz and Wagner to be the greatest innovators in the nineteenth century, from the point of view of orchestration, do you think that, compared with composers such as Schumann and Brahms, there is a difference between the way they conducted an orchestra and the way they wrote for an orchestra?

Yes and no. There are composers who have a gift for instrumental colour, for timbre, and that does not depend exclusively on how they conduct. Liszt conducted a great deal when he was at Weimar, especially the works of Wagner, but his greatest gift was writing for the piano, which went hand in hand with his pianistic virtuosity. His very first works for the piano are extremely inventive. It is therefore not so much, in my opinion, the sober and austere Liszt of the final period who is interesting, but the young Liszt who completely changed the way composers wrote for the piano, even more radically than Chopin, who, in this respect, was relatively traditional. When Liszt writes for the orchestra, it is clear that his imagination does not really take off; it is astonishing to record that, compared to Berlioz and Wagner, he is really not a genius of colour. With Mendelssohn, it is different: he knew how to use the Classical orchestra with great success and facility. The *Italian Symphony* and *A Midsummer Night's Dream* are extraordinarily well written and orchestrated – *A Midsummer Night's Dream* was, after all, written by an adolescent who had already composed a great deal. When I was in New York, I discovered some symphonies for strings written in his youth, and I conducted several of them in which it was clear that he had mastered the instrumental style. Mendelssohn was a genius of timbre, but was less inventive, less erratic than Berlioz.

Time obviously hastens development. It is not possible to compare Wagner's orchestra of 1880 with Mendelssohn's of 1840. The composers are separated by two generations, in which not only the orchestra and instrumental technique but also the instruments themselves changed. Schumann, by comparison, shows little invention and even little skill, especially in the longer works. His *Scenes from Faust* spring to mind, in which one sometimes wishes for greater colour. Put simply, there are composers who possess this gift of instrumental invention and others who, more or less, lack it. Chopin was not interested in the orchestra; Brahms was much more astute in this respect than Schumann. Yet if you compare the symphonies of Brahms with the operas of Wagner solely from the viewpoint of instrumentation, it is clear that Brahms followed Classical models, very precisely and very well, in a way that corresponds to his musical thoughts – but one is not bowled over by his instrumental imagination.

Can this difference be found with other, more recent composers?

Yes. One can compare Stravinsky's orchestral imagination with Schoenberg's. There is something in Stravinsky that calls for brilliant colour, diversity of orchestral richness almost for its own sake; he has this innate ability to use instruments as effectively as possible. With Schoenberg, the instrumental writing is very much more a function of the musical text. It makes clear how motifs and themes are related. He is, of course, fully aware of the instruments' capacity and their expressive connotations, but the way he uses them is far from merely hedonistic, as can be seen in the late works which risk falling into didacticism – whereas the earlier works, such as Op. 16 and 22, display a paradoxical richness that is both hedonistic and functional.

Being a conductor, it seems, is not enough to stimulate this inner sensitivity to sound.

No. It helps you to resolve practical problems, but that is all. Orchestral imagination is a particular gift. When Berlioz wrote the *Symphonie fantastique*, he was still very young and had very little direct experience of the orchestra. And yet in my view it was with the young Berlioz that the modern orchestra, as one perceives it now, really began. Moreover, it must be remembered that Wagner, early in his career, was greatly impressed by the virtuosity of Berlioz and was also deeply influenced by him, although of course he dismissed the picturesque side of Berlioz, about which he expressed some not very flattering views, albeit after the composer's death. And then, it must not be forgotten that Berlioz had been far from generous to Wagner at the time of the *Tannhäuser* scandal – personal grievances, therefore, played their part.

Could you summarize what you consider to be modern in the orchestration of these two composers?

With Berlioz, there are a number of obvious characteristics. Although he derives from Beethoven, he uses features that run counter to the rules of composition in general, such as the chords in close position in the low register of the double basses at the beginning of the 'March to the Scaffold' in the *Symphonie fantastique*. They are nothing more than triads – nothing could be more traditional – but in this register, with those instruments, with this type of playing (pizzicato), it has more to do with the composite timbre than a simple triad. Similarly, his use of kettledrums at the end of the 'Pastoral' movement is, harmonically, very blurred – literally unclassifiable, but it produces a sound that is quite remarkable for its time. These are some of the elements of his musical vocabulary which are highly original. And the use of extreme registers in the *Requiem* – trombones deep in the bass, flutes in the treble and nothing in between – produces something very strange that I find again in certain Debussy *Préludes*, where the left hand deep in the bass and the right hand high in the treble play parallel chords. Likewise, towards the end of the first movement of Mahler's Ninth Symphony, there is a passage for flute, horn, cellos and double basses where the combination of instruments dissolves the texture of the ensemble and is reduced to three

44

lines floating in a harmonic void. It's interesting to note that such things can also be observed in Berlioz, but his awkwardnesses, his harmonic blunders, prove that in this area his imagination is not as strong as his originality vis-à-vis timbre.

Which was not the case with Wagner . . .

Ah no! Wagner continued to develop. If you compare the harmony of *Der fliegende Holländer* with that of *Parsifal*, you are faced with two very different worlds. Whereas if you look at the late works of Berlioz, the picturesque side often vies with the neo-Classical. His thinking is weaker, less acute than it was. This can clearly be seen in the dances of *Les Troyens*, the least convincing part of the work.

Wagner was none the less inspired by Berlioz.

He was struck by the richness of his orchestral imagination. He recognizes as much in *Roméo et Juliette*. But Wagner's orchestration developed at the same time as his polyphony. The more he refined his use of the leitmotiv – *Götterdämmerung* is in this respect exceptional – the more different his orchestration became. When he came to compose *Parsifal*, he admitted that he would have liked an orchestra twice the normal size to express his thoughts as he wished. I also have a Utopian ideal – it remains nothing more than that – to have an orchestra made up of complete families of instruments: all the flutes, from the piccolo to the bass flute; all the oboes, including the oboe d'amore, the baritone, etc. The clarinets get closest to this ideal since they provide every register, from the E flat clarinet to the contrabass. But that would mean having a similar number of strings –

something that Berlioz suggests at the end of his *Treatise on Orchestration*. He imagines what he calls his festival orchestra, which would result in the most incredible sounds imaginable. He describes his Utopia in detail and reveals, a little like Sade planning the end of *Cent Vingt Journées*, the infinite possibilities and combinations that could be offered with additional orchestras of harps, cellos, pianos and other tubas. But no festival has yet made this fabulous prospect a reality.

Mahler and Strauss:
two great elder statesmen

We know that Berlioz fulminated against the practice of modifying Beethoven's symphonies – but Mahler was later to renew this practice; he modified not only Beethoven but also Schumann, I think. How do we view this practice today?

Berlioz did not object to the orchestration of a work being modified, but rather to a work being massacred, which is quite different. He cites the trio in the scherzo of Beethoven's Fifth Symphony, where the double basses are required to play in unison with the cellos – which must indeed have been difficult at the time – and he describes how the double bass players, not wishing to expose themselves to this peril, simply stopped playing. He was naturally outraged by this type of solution by default. Double bass players were certainly not great virtuosi when Berlioz was young; and they were still likened not long ago to water carriers. But from Mahler on, there could no longer be any question of semi-amateurs in an orchestra. There is, however, a practical reason for these modifications; instruments evolve (e.g. chromatic brass), balance changes (with the enlargement of the orchestra) and composers – Schumann, for example – can write clumsily. Today, great store is set by authenticity, by recreating the exact conditions of a particular era; to a certain extent, that can be a good thing, because in that way the score is protected from outrageous distortions. But such a pursuit of authenticity can also be rather pointless; it is wishful thinking to recreate the past exactly.

Instruments in Berlioz's time were more limited and had weaknesses, and the concert halls were generally smaller. Imagine Beethoven symphonies performed in the auditorium of the old Conservatoire in Paris, with approximately six hundred seats! I heard Charles Munch conduct concerts in this hall during the war; the stage was easily large enough for a Classical orchestra. The three horns of the *Eroica* sounded 'spectacular' in such a setting. In the nineteenth century, especially from 1870–80 onwards, larger auditoria were gradually built. There was an enormous expansion of culture in middle-class society, particularly musical culture, and the capacity of these halls soon exceeded 1,500, 1,600 places and eventually reached 2,000. There is no doubt that acoustically the orchestra as Beethoven knew it sounded relatively puny in these new spaces and, to Mahler's mind, did not correspond to the grandiose inspiration of the music. It should also be added that Mahler's concept of Beethoven was seen through the distorting lens of Wagner's music. Beethoven's actual sound seemed to Mahler insufficient, compared with the sound as he imagined it.

Another way of putting it is like this: the composer took into consideration the conditions of his own time, but if he had had better conditions, he would have eagerly accepted them. There are letters in which Mozart expresses his satisfaction at not being restricted to a small number of strings but having a large number at his disposal. To dismiss *a priori* a larger number of musicians is not only dogmatic but fails to take into account the possibility of adapting the practices of the past.

Another element explains why Mahler altered Beethoven's scores: namely, the characteristics of certain instruments of the time in which the works were written. Beethoven only had natural horns at his disposal, since valve horns were a later invention. Berlioz himself, in *Roméo et Juliette*, always uses natural horns, whose limitations he attempts to overcome, and with which, through acrobatic combinations, he strives to obtain a harmony that corresponds to the treatment of the chromatic instruments of his orchestra. At the beginning of the last movement of Beethoven's Ninth, the natural horns have a 'clash' of a semitone (B flat against A) with the rest of the orchestra. What can be done today? Be true to Beethoven and preserve the so-called clash, or 'correct' the brass – in other words, adjust the score according to the instruments' present-day capabilities? The problem can only be resolved according to whether one has faith in authenticity or in going beyond the limitations of the period. Mahler's modifications can be justified in view of the changing situation. None the less, the question still remains: do you confine the works to the period in which they were created, or do you bring them nearer to us through subsequently acquired means. If you concentrate on the past, you can only achieve a reconstruction; if you concentrate on the present, betrayals. The choice can therefore only be between two falsifications. I remember hearing the orchestral changes that Georg Szell brought to the symphonies of Schumann. They were undertaken in the spirit of Mahler, to smooth over the awkwardnesses, the flaws in balance and the clumsy writing. Schumann submitted his orchestral scores to Mendelssohn, who didn't hesitate to correct the orchestration. It is tempting to think that, in this case, it was the academician correcting the genius, but in fact it was simply that the flaws in Schumann's instrumental technique often stem from a weakness as much of imagination as of the means to realize it. There is no need to distort the score when one can be absolutely sure about its authenticity. At the beginning of the first movement of Debussy's *La mer*, the strings cover the whole register, while the main part is given to a bassoon solo. If you have only a single bassoonist, he is obliged to play loudly to make himself heard, and this detracts from the 'sweet and expressive' sentiment that the composer wanted. Isn't it better to have two bassoons playing this *piano* dynamic as marked, in order to keep the required timbre and maintain the balance with the strings? In a case like this, I find such an initiative is far from sacrilege.

As for Mahler, he was always correcting his own scores. Isn't it true that these modifications came from his experience as a conductor?

When you write an orchestral score, you can make mistakes, even if you have absolute mastery, especially if you compose by referring to your past experience. The composer only hears an approximation of what he seeks, and he is sometimes disappointed because the difference is too great between the imagined and the real sound – which can lead to self-reproach. Mahler, as far as I know, never changed his own orchestration, although he changed quite a few other details that didn't satisfy him. Debussy too. Sometimes, even in Mahler's case, you should not trust impulsive corrections, since they might have been dictated by irritation or in a fit of bad temper after an inadequate or poor performance. When I was involved in preparing the critical edition of Debussy's *Jeux*, I noticed a passage in which he cut the bassoons – which deprives the music of a colour and harmony which to me seem indispensable. Perhaps during a rehearsal these three bassoonists had been unable to play at the dynamic level required by the composer, who then, no doubt, expressed his dissatisfaction – which is not sufficient justification for such a cut. Other corrections, as in the third *Nocturne* ('Sirens'), are completely justified because they lighten or improve the balance of certain passages. The end result corresponds better to the musical thought. It should not be forgotten that a work can sound different when played by different instrumentalists in an auditorium with a different acoustic. The difference need not be great, but a horn can sometimes benefit from a lively acoustic and at other times from a less reverberant one – which can, for example, change the balance of a chord. The solutions, whether they have to do with the acoustic or the actual music, are as varied as the situations in which you find yourself.

Yes, but with Mahler, this correcting of his own scores was almost an obsession. Das Lied von der Erde *and the* Ninth Symphony *were not corrected because they were not played in his lifetime. Do you think he would have corrected them, too?*

I cannot quite envisage what alterations he would have made – perhaps a reinforcement here or, conversely, the removal of a doubling, or even . . . It should also be noted that some composers – Stravinsky, for example – almost never corrected their scores. It's true that he reorchestrated entire works such as *Petrushka* and *The Firebird* or the *Symphonies of wind instruments*, but that was a question of producing a new version, not making the occasional correction. Nor did Ravel correct his scores, with the sole exception of *Une barque sur l'océan*, which he was not satisfied with – goodness knows why; the work, in my view, is a perfect masterpiece.

It is said that there are composers who have an immediate and intuitive grasp of musical balance.

Yes, it's impressive to see how Wagner, for example, produces balance in his works. He is a true genius in this respect, undeniably so, even down to working out almost the exact number of instruments. I'm fascinated by the precision with which Wagner gauges orchestral balance. The *Ring*, a work of great length and breadth, contains a multiplicity of details that are achieved with astonishing precision. Nietzsche said that Wagner was a master of the miniature, and this was certainly not meant as praise. To my way of thinking, however, it is a great compliment; the orchestral detail strengthens the great sweep of the work. This problem of balancing detail and ensemble in an acceptable way is precisely what makes Wagner, in my view, so challenging for the performer.

Strauss, unlike Berlioz or even Wagner, never mentions the exact number of instruments required; he simply writes 'at least 21 first violins, at least 18 second violins'. He seems to allow the conductor greater freedom.

Strauss indicates what he considers to be the ideal number of strings to balance this section of the orchestra with the other instrumental groups. Still, I suppose that with his experience and pragmatism he was persuaded to accept slightly different numbers, albeit within certain limits. It comes down in the end to the size of the orchestra pit. Strauss was not, I think, obsessed with numbers, and he knew how to balance his musical thoughts with the means he had at his disposal. Paul Sacher told me that when he commissioned *Metamorphosen*, Strauss asked him: 'How many strings do you have?' 'Twenty-three!' And he kept to these twenty-three strings. He knew how to adapt, and he could use the orchestra with exceptional virtuosity.

I believe you have seen Strauss conduct on film.

Yes, filmed on two different occasions. The first was between 1933 and 1934 in Vienna, when he was still in good health. The second was during a gala in Munich in celebration of his eighty-fifth birthday, shortly before he died. On the first occasion, he looked to be in excellent health, and although his gestures were limited, he was completely in control. On the second occasion, when he conducted a scene from *Der Rosenkavalier*, he no longer had the physical energy of the earlier years, but you still had the feeling that he was utterly in control. He indicated the entries with the smallest of gestures, but these were extraordinarily effective. Given the circumstances, of course, I imagine that everyone was aware of the slightest wink, the slightest nuance. What you observe, however, is a professional who, despite his failing strength, was a complete master of his trade. No one who saw him conduct Mozart's operas at Salzburg, especially between the wars, has ever forgotten it. He also gave advice to young conductors, fairly sarcastic advice, saying, for instance, that it was not the conductor who should sweat but the audience!

You have never conducted the operas of Richard Strauss. Why?

Quite simply because Wieland Wagner died too early, as I've already said.

How would you define Mahler's orchestration, compared to Strauss's?

One thing is clear: technically, they are equals. Strauss's orchestration is quite brilliant, but his symphonic works are less rich in development and ideas than Mahler's.

Do you not think that Mahler stands somewhere between Wagner and the composers of the Second Viennese School?

Certainly. Works such as Schoenberg's *Gurrelieder* continue the tradition not only of Mahler, but also of Strauss and Wagner.

I was thinking of Webern when I asked you this question.

Webern represents a sort of distillation of this tradition. None the less, he too employed a vast orchestra at the outset of his career. In the first version of Op. 6, he used an exceptional amount of brass – six trombones, for example, to create homogenous chords – but also instruments that were little used at that time, such as the alto flute and the E flat clarinet, which allowed him to extend the traditional registers of any given timbre. Mahler never used the alto flute, but he made extensive use of the E flat clarinet. His orchestration reveals a tremendous imagination: a variety of timbres, a wealth of different combinations, confidence in the use of registers, all contributing to extremely vivid results. The composers of the Second Viennese School were later to benefit from this example, while looking at the same time for solutions that were more in keeping with the particular character of their own musical ideas.

Mahler and Strauss were both great conductors. But Mahler, unlike Strauss, did not compose operas, though he conducted many.

Perhaps he had seen the disagreeable side, the everyday difficulties of opera, but perhaps also he was more attracted by a pure theatre of the imagination. There are certain moments when you can see that his dramatic imagination was fuelled more by symphonic ambitions than it could have been by theatre.

As a conductor, how do you assess the question of balance in the scores of Mahler and Strauss?

There is never anything to correct in their scores. Not only do they have an innate sense of the orchestra, they can also draw on what they themselves experienced daily from a very early age. Although Strauss's music, like Mahler's, can be dense and closely worked, both composers are realistic in their demands. The dynamic markings of a work like Berg's Op. 6, on the other hand, occasionally have to be corrected, otherwise it would lack clarity. This is particularly true in the complex polyphony of the third movement, where the main voices and the secondary voices need to be clarified to be heard as such.

You mean that the notation is not precise enough in this sense . . .

It is merely insufficient. You sometimes need to alter the dynamics to bring out the hierarchy of the voices. Curiously enough, Berg's first work, the *Altenberg-Lieder*, poses no problem: there is nothing to correct, it is wonderfully orchestrated. His cantata *Der Wein*, a late work, shows less invention; likewise *Lulu*, which seems to me, from this point of view, less inventive than *Wozzeck*, which was composed earlier.

Amongst those composers who are renowned for their skill in orchestration, where do you place Debussy?

Debussy is, in this respect, less 'sure' than Ravel, but his use of the orchestra extends his musical invention and enriches it. Ravel is infallible; he assembles, as it were, a score that has already been entirely worked out – which explains the constant interchange between piano and orchestral versions; and why he is so skilled in transfiguring the music of Mussorgsky, while remaining faithful to the text. There are no mistakes either with Stravinsky or Webern, but their textures, it must be said, are simpler than Berg's.

Stravinsky's performances of his own works

The case of Stravinsky is quite different, because he was a composer who was not really a conductor and who only conducted his own works.

No, he wasn't really a conductor. I had the opportunity of seeing Stravinsky towards the end of his life, when physically he was no longer so robust. Strauss, despite the decline in his physical powers, had an absolute mastery of his craft. The older Stravinsky became, the less he could rely on a professional technique. I imagine that when he was younger, his personality overcame his technical shortcomings; when an orchestra saw him arrive, they knew that this was the composer of the *The Rite of Spring*, of *Petrushka* and *The Firebird*. His personality alone inspired great respect.

You invited him to conduct for the Domaine Musicale.

Yes, twice, and each time to conduct the first Paris performance of his own works: *Agon* in 1957 and *Threni* in 1958. What struck me was that while conducting he lost control, no doubt through anxiety, of the rhythmic pulse which is an essential element of his works. Composers do not necessarily make good conductors – the two gifts are completely different. Strauss and Mahler were equally gifted as composers and conductors; the same cannot be said, if we are to believe contemporary accounts, of Debussy and Ravel. You can be a composer of genius yet lack the ability to conduct. Messiaen never for a moment claimed that he could conduct.

As for Stravinsky, it was largely his own works that he conducted. He said that only his interpretations were valid. Do you think that as a conductor he brought something to the interpretation of his own music?

I think we are dealing here with an illusion nourished by a sort of frustration. It was not really jealousy; his personality was of a completely different order. He did, however, have this instinctive reaction to those individuals who appropriated his work and made it their own. A perfectly normal reaction if you think of the ideal of objectivity, the refusal to 'interpret' that characterized the inter-war period. Ravel was no less radical in this respect. A saying of his, made during that time, springs to mind: 'My music does not need to be interpreted, it needs to be played.'

Stravinsky's need to conduct his own music is perhaps linked to the rhythmic complexity of works like The Rite of Spring *or* Les noces. *These scores forced conductors of that period to consider adopting a different style of beat. Stravinsky was not always satisfied with the way his works were conducted. Do you think this might have been one of the things that encouraged him to conduct?*

He certainly wasn't satisfied with certain performances. He expressed particular reservations about German orchestras regarding rhythmic attack, if I can put it like that – which at the time sparked off a short-lived debate. It is true that Stravinsky's use of rhythm has implications for how the rhythm is both felt and produced which are fundamentally

foreign to the German tradition. Conductors like Furtwängler, who in a different sphere was touched with genius,
could not have felt very much at ease in the music of
Stravinsky or Bartók. Owing to his education, Furtwängler
was unable to master the irregular time signatures, which
are one of the cornerstones of this type of rhythmic invention. I am not speaking about Furtwängler conducting
Stravinsky in general, but rather about his conducting *The
Rite of Spring*. And Charles Munch, who was also brought
up in the German tradition, springs to mind. I found his
performance of *The Rite of Spring* in 1946 unconvincing.
It's not just a question of generation, because Ansermet,
who belonged to the same generation as Munch and
Désormière, had no problems conducting works of this
kind. It's clearly a question of musical education and individual personalities.

*But in what way was this Romantic style of conducting no
longer suited to the music of Stravinsky?*

There is a fundamental difference, because both Classical
and Romantic music are based on a regular metre, in units
of two, three or four, even if varied with a certain flexibility. From Stravinsky and Bartók on, you are dealing with a
metre that can be irregular – in other words, the basic pulse
consists of sometimes two, sometimes three beats with,
within one bar, every combination which that implies. One
must acquire the basic reflex that enables you to move
instantaneously from one type of metre to another. If you
have been brought up in a tradition of regularity, it can be
difficult to adapt to irregularity, especially when, past a certain age, such a reflex is more difficult to acquire.

Yes, but Stravinsky, who only conducted his own music, ought to have had the ability to conduct his own scores, because it was he who wrote them.

But who says that, if you compose a piano concerto – even one that is very well written for the instrument – you can actually play it? It's exactly the same thing. If you haven't got the necessary technique, you will not be able to play it. Ravel, who wrote his G major Piano Concerto for himself to perform during a tour of America, quickly realized that he would not be able to. And although it is not a work of great difficulty, compared to concertos by Liszt or Brahms, he entrusted it to Marguerite Long. It is clearly not the case that, because a composer writes with skill for an instrument, he will be the perfect interpreter. It would be the same as saying that, to be a good orchestrator, you would need to play the piccolo, the clarinet, the drums or the double bass – which is clearly absurd.

In which case, there is no great interest in letting a composer conduct his own works if he hasn't the skill to do so.

It's interesting to see a composer grapple with his own work. There's almost a documentary side to it, for despite everything, he gives a personal impetus to the work. And then, whenever an orchestra is confronted by a composer of Stravinsky's calibre – even if that produces tensions – it is undeniable that the players will show a certain respect and goodwill. That can sometimes produce some very beautiful and intense moments, but it can also produce moments that border on the catastrophic.

And yet Stravinsky really did say that only his interpreta-

tions were authentic; he was truly obsessive on the subject.

We're dealing here with a generation preoccupied with the notion of 'objective' performances. The personality of the performer must not come between the score and the audience; it must limit itself to transmitting the written message without any distortion. Such an attitude was clearly engendered by a generation of performers towards the end of the Romantic period, who took such liberties with the score as to render it absurd.

The interpretations of certain pianists between 1900 and 1910, preserved on piano rolls, seem rather aberrant to us because they take such liberties with rhythm, phrasing and tempo. I suppose that it was against these exaggerated interpretations that the generation of Ravel and Stravinsky rebelled. But if we look at the problem more closely, it is clear that fidelity to the text also has its limits. There exist in music many parameters that have never been written down, and never can be. A score, in short, is the noting down of a certain number of values concerning pitch, rhythm and dynamics, etc. The quantitative relationships meticulously noted down by the composer are then modified by the performer. Whether he emphasizes an accent, a phrase, a timbre, or adjusts to the acoustics of the hall or the characteristics of the instrument, he will distort the notated text and continually impose minute variations on the printed score. The illusion of the performer's objectivity is above all a reaction to aberrations of the recent past, but it has no validity in itself – except perhaps to condemn distortion. There is, moreover, no rigidly measurable tempo in music, but, rather, a supple psychological tempo; nor is there such a thing as an absolute dynamic, but only relative values. I could continue the list and come to the conclusion that, in the face of historical relativity, nothing, absolutely nothing can be rigorously or authentically objective.

Stravinsky could not have always conducted his pieces in the same way.

You only have to compare the different recordings he made of the same piece. What do you see? A personality that changes. I change too: my recordings clearly show a development. It is good that we change, because music is organic and cannot be reproduced mechanically like a photocopy.

The striking thing about Stravinsky is the way he changes style while remaining recognizably himself.

Absolutely. It stems most of all from the way he uses rhythm. His inventiveness in this area makes him write for instruments in a certain way. I do not, incidentally, believe that instrumentation can be divorced from the act of composition itself.

But his most striking works, from the point of view of orchestration, are none the less from the Ballets russes period.

The most imaginative work, as regards orchestration, still seems to me to be *The Firebird*. The language of *The Rite of Spring* is much more personal, but the orchestration is dictated by the music in the most direct possible way. *The Firebird* proceeds from a way of writing, as it were, in perspective, an acoustical style of orchestration with the same musical images superimposed in different guises. Stravinsky's model for this was Rimsky-Korsakov or Scriabin. The orchestra of *Petrushka*, though, and even more that of *The Rite of Spring*, is already typically his own. There is no longer any question of influence. The musical invention in *The Firebird* is very beautiful, but one recognizes the source. The orchestral invention is superior to the music itself, while in *The Rite of Spring* the musical inspiration and the orchestration are on the same level.

You first conducted The Rite of Spring *in 1963. Has your interpretation changed since then?*

I have recorded *The Rite of Spring* three times, at different stages in my conducting career; curiously enough, it was not *The Rite* that launched my career as a conductor but Bartók's *The Miraculous Mandarin*, which I conducted in 1959 in Donaueschingen and Aix-en-Provence. It was in July 1959 that I stood in for Hans Rosbaud (as I've already mentioned), and it was with this concert that I made my name as a conductor. In the meantime, I had begun to conduct orchestras in Holland and Germany.

I conducted my first *Rite of Spring* in Montreal with the Radio Canada Symphony Orchestra, for a television broadcast of a Canadian composer called Pierre Mercure. I already knew the score like the back of my hand; I had studied it with Olivier Messiaen, and I had analysed its rhythm in a long article and played it on the piano in a version for four hands. I was then asked to conduct *The Rite* for the fiftieth anniversary of its first performance in June 1963, and I made it a point of honour to conduct it without the score, since conducting by heart is also a question of discipline. Of course, I embarked on this project with a certain apprehension; but it was *The Rite* that effectively launched me in France. 1963 was a decisive year for me.

Had you developed a particular way of conducting for The Rite of Spring?

No, it was my own way, but I must admit that when I listen again to the first recording with the Orchestre Nationale de France made in 1963, I find the performance very tense. I was concentrating so hard on not making mistakes that I was a bag of nerves. I then played *The Rite* again with the Cleveland Orchestra and I felt much more at ease. I often played the work with this orchestra, especially when touring university towns, and I recorded it again after one of these tours during 1967–8, and felt much more secure, in much greater control of the score. But four years had passed.

If one compares these three recordings, can a development be detected in your interpretation?

I've certainly gained a greater control of things, because I listen more; then there's the difference the orchestra makes, and the Cleveland Orchestra is absolutely first class. Above all, I think I've changed in the way I get the work across, not in my conception of it. I look at this work in the way I did when I studied it in 1945–6, that's to say, well before I ever planned to perform it. It is not possible to alter much in Stravinsky, whereas with Debussy my relationship has changed in a more obvious way, acquiring, I suppose, more flexibility and intuition.

Webern as conductor

In your complete recording of the works of Webern, you insisted on including his orchestration of Schubert's German Dances, *conducted by Webern himself. What was the reason for this choice?*

I wanted to conduct the *German Dances* myself, since we were recording all of Webern's works, but when I was told that there was a recording of him conducting them, I felt this would be interesting, especially as it was a rare example of him as a performer, and would show how he thought of Schubert's music, with which for many reasons he had an affinity.

And what do you think of this recording?

I was very surprised, above all by his use of rubato, which can appear mannered today but which seems natural to him. Had this recording been made by any other composer at the beginning of the century, one would have expected this type of articulation, but for such a composer, celebrated for his rigour and indeed asceticism, to play like this at the very time he was composing his Op. 21 and Op. 24, seems at first quite incomprehensible. A possible but not very probable explanation is that it provided a relaxing contrast to his asceticism. Or did he perhaps think of all music, including his own, in this way? Perhaps such devices were, in his eyes, essential to expressiveness. Universal Edition have published a facsimile of the Op. 27 *Variations* for piano that belonged to Peter Stadlen, the Austrian pianist, which includes Webern's own markings. Above almost every note there is a little expressive swell, and in almost every bar a *ritardando*. This results in a piece in which rigour and strong emotion constantly coexist. Webern was certainly keen on this sort of expressiveness. At first, it can seem strange, but when you think about it, you begin to understand better this quintessential emotiveness, which transfigures the rigour of his formal structures.

Especially when you are dealing with a work as austere as these Variations . . .

Yes, but today, with hindsight, we can better appreciate the expressiveness of this work, which was not understood in 1945. What struck one at the time, above all at the structural level, was the radical reform of the musical language. And sometimes the reception of these works was also fairly radical, overlooking everything about the music that was traditional. In fact, the music is much more emotional in essence than was thought at the time. Personally, I now play Webern with far greater flexibility than I used to. I've come to see the importance of this understanding – for Webern, the emotional range was as much a part of his musical conception as the structural design. One must keep the continuity of line, even across silences, interruptions, disjunctions. In the period between 1940 and 1950, I heard some terribly unsatisfactory performances of the *Symphony* Op. 21. I really would not like to hear them again today. Musicians have developed so much in the last forty years, and now have a clearer understanding of the text. Performers understand their role within the continuity of a phrase, even if they only have a few notes to play, separated by intervals of silence. The structural design must be transformed into actions, into 'speaking' gestures. But in a more spontaneous work, such as the *Five Pieces for Orchestra* Op. 10, everything must be in place with the same precision – which would tend to prove that, whether the writing be free or strict, it is the expression which is both its impulse and its goal.

III

The Founding of the EIC and IRCAM

The founding of the EIC and the choice of repertoire

You founded the EIC in 1976, at the instigation of Michel Guy. Your idea at the outset was to create a large orchestra, which was then reduced in size . . .

No. That's not quite right. When I founded IRCAM [Institut de recherche et de coordination acoustique/ musique: Institute for Acoustic and Musical Research and Coordination] at about the same time, I realized that we were going to commission works which, in order to be played in public, would require a group of performers. The ensemble Musique Vivante, which could have taken part in such performances, was too unpredictable: the players were not employed full-time; they also belonged to other groups and had other obligations, which meant that they could not be relied upon to appear at every rehearsal. It was impossible, therefore, to guarantee the total freedom of movement which seemed to me necessary. Having spent time in America and England, where I had benefited from excellent working conditions, I had no wish to come up against the sort of conditions I had encountered when I was much younger. It was necessary to create for contemporary music exactly the same conditions as for a repertory orchestra, albeit with more flexibility and adaptability. After discussions with Michel Guy, it was decided to found the Ensemble InterContemporain. With the help of Nicholas Snowman, we tried to define the ideal size of the ensemble and also, within the ensemble, the right proportion of woodwind, brass, strings, percussion and keyboard instruments. To this end, Nicholas studied a large part of the twentieth-century repertoire down to the present era, which enabled us to define – statistically, as it were – the composition of the ensemble: double woodwind (plus a bass clarinet), a group of brass instruments similarly constituted, a string section with three violins, two violas, two cellos and a double bass, three keyboard players (celesta, harmonium, synthesizer), a harp and three percussionists. That seemed to be, if not the ideal formation, at least the most practical for playing a fairly large repertoire. The intention, of course, was not to restrict the ensemble to this formation, but to add players when necessary; the essential thing was to have a permanent nucleus of players. We then decided to form another ensemble with particular emphasis on the strings which, in the EIC, had not been very numerous compared to the other sections. The idea was to form a homogenous ensemble of strings, with a few woodwind and brass players and a timpanist – in other words, a small Classical ensemble that is usually called a Mozartian ensemble.

There were two ensembles, then . . .

Yes, two independent ensembles which could, for certain programmes, combine as a single orchestra. It is very difficult for the EIC to play a work that requires a considerable number of strings – extra players need to be recruited individually. It turned out that the Ministry of Culture lacked the necessary funds to achieve this end; the City of Paris, however, decided at the same moment to create an ensemble of this type, which then became the Ensemble Orchestral de Paris.

You became interested in another project.

Yes, but they were two completely different ensembles. We gave some concerts together, but as there were two different artistic managements, two totally different methods of recruitment, it could never really work.

How did you set about recruiting? An ensemble that is devoted entirely to contemporary music presupposes that the players have a certain commitment . . .

The fact that the players applied to join the EIC indicates that they were interested in contemporary music. Besides, we made no secret of our aims: the players who applied were in full knowledge of the facts. At the outset, it's true, there were rumours that it would be a deluxe ensemble whose players would be very well paid and do very little – which was not at all, of course, our intention. We did, however, decide to engage most of the players on two-thirds time, which is still the case today, so that they would not be exclusively taken up with twentieth-century music and could each do the necessary, indeed essential, preparation before ensemble rehearsals began; they would also have time to concentrate on others areas of music – something that we most certainly did not deny them. That was an enrichment and meant that they developed different points of view, different instrumental techniques. I was keen to establish and respect this principle right from the beginning: that most of their time should be devoted to the repertoire of the EIC, but not all of it.

And as for recruiting players . . .

We auditioned them in the traditional way. The one thing I introduced regarding decision-making was a result of my experiences in America: the Musical Director – in the case of the EIC, the President (myself) – has the casting vote. The jury is present in an advisory capacity, and plays a crucial role in expressing the opinion it is called upon to give, but the final decision is made by the President alone. The responsibility of the final choice is his.

Yours, in other words.

Yes, mine. I think it is better like that, because it avoids all sorts of compromise. But of course, I always take into account the views of the players, for they are more familiar with the specific technique of their own instruments than I am. But an instrumental player does not necessarily have a sufficiently overall view, and he will often restrict himself to those areas of activity with which he is familiar. That is why a conductor's experience is of great value, because it permits him to assess the candidates' potential and their ability to enrich the existing ensemble. Personally, I tend to prefer a player who has more potential to one who has already fulfilled that potential. I have taken risks, of course, but I have rarely made mistakes. I have even on occasions recruited players who had never been engaged before and who, at nineteen or twenty, had just finished their studies. At that age and, of course, with talent, they are very malleable and can be moulded, which is more difficult with older players. I do not systematically choose them because they are young, but neither do I baulk at doing so. If an instrumentalist has talent, I disregard his or her lack of experience.

They gradually acquire experience.

They acquire it continuously, according to the works they encounter. My task is to make sure they acquire it.

The auditions, it seems, are very difficult and long.

Yes, they can sometimes last for fifty minutes. It's a gruelling test for the candidate and the jury, but we have not found a form of recruitment that is better or fairer. There are two stages: the preliminary stage is presided over by the Musical Director, the final stage by me. The candidates first play a Classical piece which allows us to assess their intonation, style, virtuosity and mastery of their instrument, but also establishes the essential relationship between the standard repertoire and new works. They then play a contemporary work of their own choice, which allows us to discover their personal predilections. That is, for me, a decisive factor in assessing the character and profile of a musician. The candidates must then choose from four set contemporary pieces – which allows them to select the piece that best suits their temperament. They then play one or two extracts from a twentieth-century classic; and finally there is a sight-reading test. When all the candidates have been considered, the jury – which represents all sections of the orchestra, with players of the candidate's own instrument predominating – then starts its discussions. I've observed that the auditions give rise to a great deal of subjective judgements, especially where the strings are concerned, whether the auditions take place at the Ensemble, in New York or in London. Someone will say: 'Remarkable bow technique but faulty intonation'; someone else: 'Perfect intonation but bow technique a little stiff'. You ask yourself whether you've heard the same player. Why this disparity? There are many types of different bow techniques and different stylistic approaches which stem not only from the teacher but, more generally, from a country, from a certain school of playing. You must take note of opinions but place them in context; it's a skill one acquires. Sometimes you just have to take a line; but collectively, with the changes of view brought about by our sometimes very animated discussions, we relatively seldom make the wrong choice. Mistakes, however, can never be discounted.

Objectives and programming

The Ensemble, then, was formed. But other ensembles already existed, such as the Musique Vivante, the 2e2m, L'Itinéraire and Ars Nova – groups of freelance players which had for many years been programming concerts of a great variety of contemporary music. How did your first objectives differ from what they were doing?

There were three kinds of objective. The first was to assimilate thoroughly the repertoire of the first half of the twentieth century. That seemed to me very important: it is impossible to play new music well if you have not assimilated the musical language that went before. You cannot with impunity pass from Haydn to Stockhausen without being familiar with Schoenberg or Webern, for example. Notions of intonation, rhythm and ensemble are different, by virtue of the evolution of musical language. It was necessary, therefore, for these so-called 'twentieth-century classics' to be played often, and that they should be considered to be the basic repertoire and the reference point for both the Ensemble and the public. In the repertoire of the nineteenth century, the technical problems are reckoned to be known, likewise matters of style; it is, above all, individual interpretations that are open to question – whereas in a new work, players encounter technical difficulties and characteristics of style at the same time. That inevitably creates an obstacle to be overcome.

The second objective was discovery: to play new, recently composed works, to rehearse them with sufficient time and in good conditions. As with the classics, it is essential to play new works sufficiently often to create a cohesive ensemble and a style of performance. We try to reprogramme works so that the players feel increasingly at ease, no longer consider the pieces an effort to play, but feel at home with a familiar language in which they can express themselves with a certain freedom. Selection, of course, comes into play, and it quickly becomes clear that some of the new works are more significant than others.

The third objective was the players' relationship with IRCAM – in other words, the relationship between their instrument and technology. There is, of course, nothing obligatory about this, and not all musicians are equally interested in what today's technology can bring to their own instrument, but it is vital that some of them find themselves in sympathy with IRCAM and take part in the experiments carried out there.

There is, however, a fourth objective which only came later, since there was neither room nor place for it at the outset: education. It can be viewed from three different angles. Firstly, from the perspective of the players, who give lessons to young students finishing their studies so that they can master the current techniques for playing specific pieces and learn how to integrate in the group. The second point concerns conducting, since young conductors almost never have the opportunity of conducting an orchestra, because of the expense. Thirdly, teaching also concerns composers. Young composers, still attending composition classes, also very rarely have the opportunity of hearing their works played by professional ensembles. Works by students are most frequently performed by students and conducted by students – which means that there can be no high-quality performance, since all three partners are in the process of discovering a new universe, and they do not necessarily discover it in the same way and at the same moment. We have been gradually developing the educational side since we've been at the Cité de la Musique at La Villette, and more specifically during the twentieth-century summer academies and the events undertaken in collaboration with the Paris Conservatoire.

Let us return to programming the twentieth-century classics. You could not play everything. You had to make a selection.

Some things were more pressing than others. I tried at first to give a coherence to the ensemble, musically speaking. The great classics include, of course, the substantial repertoire of the three Viennese, a small number of works by Stravinsky, Bartók's *Village Scenes*, which are, however, written for chorus and ensemble, and many of his chamber-music pieces, which do not require a conductor, that are an essential part of his œuvre. Varèse, too, was performed a great deal, because the forces he generally employs correspond in size exactly to those of the EIC. I should like to add that we promoted chamber music that did not need a conductor – Bartók, for example – as much as the conducted repertoire. It is essential for the group as a whole to be enriched by each individual contribution – that is a vital part of chamber music.

As for more contemporary chamber music, there are rather marginal trends, such as minimalism, that you have not played much.

We have played the minimalists, but I cannot personally

show much interest in this sort of music. I do not, however, put forward my own personal tastes when it comes to programming. Steve Reich, for example, has been performed very frequently by David Robertson, because he is very fond of Reich's music.

And Xenakis . . .

Xenakis was played during the first few seasons with great regularity. I myself conducted *Jalons*, a piece that was commissioned for the tenth anniversary of the EIC. Composers from my own generation who were regularly performed included Berio, Birtwistle, Donatoni, Kagel, Kurtág, Ligeti, Maderna, Nono, Pousseur, Stockhausen, Zimmermann . . . Messiaen, too, was frequently performed. Likewise Dallapiccola and Petrassi. I don't think that many important names slipped through our net.

And what about music theatre?

I can't say that it's a great passion of mine, the few works I've seen have not really convinced me, except Ligeti's *Aventures* and *Nouvelles aventures* that were played a few times, but that's more like a concert situation veering towards the absurd. I honestly think that no one of this generation has been neglected. We also set out to discover new talent: Manoury, Dalbavie, Hurel, Durieux, Benjamin, Rihm and many others . . . We are always on the lookout for new talent.

Did you have the impression at the very beginning that the public was still virginal? That your concerts were responding to a very strong demand?

When we began, groups that already existed were finding it difficult to survive; the working conditions, as I've explained, were inadequate. It was not the lack of talent but the poor working conditions that failed to generate quality. When Michel Guy looked at these problems head on, he realized that the present deficiencies would have to be remedied by improving these conditions. Of course, my return to France also played a small part. The concerts were from the outset very well attended, thanks to the connection with the Centre Pompidou. A highlight of the first season was the 'Passage du XXe siècle' [Journey through the Twentieth Century], a series of concerts that defined our aims. These concerts had an immediate impact: Nicholas Snowman and Brigitte Marger helped me to create an 'event' that was crucial for the successful launch of two institutions about which there had been serious misgivings from the start. It was necessary to set a standard that was achieved thanks to numerous contributions from France and abroad. The character of these two institutions was thus clearly defined.

IRCAM: the musician and technology

IRCAM was thought of before the Ensemble InterContemporain, and goes back to 1970; one of the first objectives was to create a centre for research.

That is absolutely right, it was to be a centre of research. I had realized that research always got the smallest slice of the cake in the musical life in which I participated, whether it was in London, Cleveland or New York. Research in America was always carried out at the heart of the universities, which were, so to speak, fortresses with little contact with the outside world. In London, there was, in fact, only one centre of research, and in Germany there had been nothing really new since 1950–60. All these studios showed signs of exhaustion, depending as they did on radio organizations whose budgets decreased more and more as television developed. The studios were mere appendages of universities and radio stations, and became superfluous as soon as the economic situation worsened. I told myself that it was essential to create a single, self-contained organization. When President Pompidou invited me to become involved in the centre which now bears his name, I thought that my dreams had come true. There had already been a failed attempt in Germany with the Max Planck Foundation. It was, in fact, scientists who suggested that a Max Planck Institute for music should be founded – an institute that was to be vaster and more multifunctional than IRCAM. It was to house several different departments: education, performance, musicological research and, finally, contemporary music – a department on which I had been asked to make a report that I drafted in 1967–8. Nothing came of all this: there was a temporary recession in Germany, and other scientists, the most significant of whom was Werner Heisenberg, were not in favour of such an institute for musical research. Musical invention was, in their eyes, a matter of spontaneity, and there was no need for research of any kind. As is often the case, the musical knowledge of a scientist turns out to be extremely conventional and rather limited. I had kept my plan, telling myself that it would perhaps see the light of day some time in the future. In 1969–70, after my discussions with Georges Pompidou, I redrafted this plan in a more specific direction, because I considered it necessary to create a place where composers could work without any unacceptable constraint on either their time or their output.

Work with scientists . . .

With scientists, of course.

Did any rapprochement take place between scientists and musicians in this technological adventure? How do you see the situation today?

I've noticed that it's much more difficult than I thought for musicians and scientists to rub shoulders with one another. I've even fewer illusions on this subject than I had twenty-five years ago! There are several reasons for this. Firstly, because scientists and musicians are educated in a different way. Secondly, I think that the scientific and the musical imaginations are manifested and function in a different way – scientific intuition does not have the same starting-point as musical intuition. Thirdly, it is exceptionally rare to find individuals with both talents. If it is exceptional to find a scientist who has a deep understanding of music, it is even more exceptional to find a musician who possesses a sound knowledge of science. It would be illogical to consider such skills normal; it would be very difficult in one lifetime to absorb all the specialized information of these two areas of knowledge.

What I appreciate – and it does exist, but all too rarely – is the ability of a scientist to enter into the mind of a musician and understand not only what he wishes to do but also why he wishes to do it, and his ability to translate that into his own scientific system of thought. The reverse ought also to exist from a musician's viewpoint.

Peppino di Giugno, who created the 4X processor, told me this about certain composers: 'They are not satisfied, because they are not really aware of the possibilities of the computer; it's as if one were asking a violinist to have a hand with six or seven fingers . . .' It's true that one often comes across this attitude with musicians: they demand more, because they do not know how to use what exists. This problem was one of the difficulties that needed to be resolved: we needed to trigger not just an exchange between individuals but also between cultures; there ought to be a consolidation of more general links between scientific and musical knowledge that share common ground. At any rate, one should not be deluded into thinking that there can be an exact correlation between one domain and the other: each has its own specific parameters. An exact correlation, far from being convincing, would run the risk of being superficial and absurd.

The problem of real time

From the beginning of the 1970s, the rapid development of electronic equipment brought about the emergence of a new kind of music. Various acoustic sound sources (instrumental or vocal) could now be amplified and transformed through an electronic device in real time, i.e. during a concert performance rather than in the studio. 1981 saw the birth of the 4X, the real-time Digital Signal Processor perfected by di Giugno. And in 1990, computer science made possible the control in real time of a synthesizer by an instrument that is linked to it. Today, we speak of interactive music. Previously, electro-acoustic music for instruments and electronic sounds had to be performed on tape, on which the conductor was completely dependent. And it is clear today that one of the central themes of IRCAM was the development of real time techniques that you breathed life into . . .

That was one of my most persistent ideas, which at the outset was by no means understood by everyone. It was argued that real time could only produce token results, and would never attain the refinement and sophistication of electronic music prepared in the studio. For me, who had had the experience of working as a composer and a performer – both of my own works and those that I had conducted since 1958 – it was unremitting torture to be a composer who was entirely reliant on the guidance of a pre-recorded tape part which couldn't be altered, except in terms of secondary criteria such as dynamics or spatial layout. I found this extremely arbitrary, fundamentally anti-creative: one's concentration is focused entirely on keeping in time with the pre-recorded tape part, and the interpretation is destroyed by this obsessive activity. As the 1970s approached, it became clear to me that it was essential for the future of music to come to a union in real time between a virtual score and an instrumental score. Much that I did was with this in mind, and I had di Giugno as an ally, who shared my view entirely.

There were two opposing positions that were very marked: on the one hand, there were those researchers who gave preference to pre-recording with rather grandiose, almost cosmic projects, but from a practical viewpoint these were unrealizable; on the other hand, there was the artisan, stubborn if not hot-headed, who, on the contrary, took things in a much more pragmatic and realistic way. In the end, everything calmed down, and both sides realized that this antagonism was becoming progressively obsolete as technology was becoming more efficient. It became clear that one could from now on do almost everything in real time that one used to be able to do with pre-recording. In cases such as these, I very much believe in progress. The efficiency and the reliability of today's computers increase as their size decreases: there is no comparison between what we knew in the 1970s and what we are capable of doing today. When IRCAM was founded, I made extensive enquiries before forming an opinion. In America, I often met Max Matthews, who worked at the Bell Telephone Company. I also went to visit the studios in Stockholm and Utrecht. I then understood that we were on the threshold of a radical revolution, and that the computer was becoming an essential work tool.

From this moment on, problems must have arisen that were, from a compositional viewpoint, very different, for it was now necessary to integrate this notion of real time into the writing of a traditionally notated score.

Since everything that is new poses problems, you have to think in terms of the differences. It is, above all, the method of work, rather than the thought itself, that is different. When you write instrumental music, you extrapolate from all your previous experiences, both with reference to your own work and to the scores of the recent or distant past. That implies a knowledge of past compositions but not necessarily of performance technique. If, for example, you are writing for an oboe in an orchestral piece, it is not necessary to be familiar with the harmonic spectrum of this instrument, or how the instrument is constructed; nor are you obliged to be able to play it. These three aspects do not impinge directly on your creative process. You must, on the other hand, be familiar with the instrument's sound quality, its volume vis-à-vis register, agility of articulation, expressive power . . . In the end, you avail yourself of these elements, according to an aesthetic aim. It is no different with technology. I am certainly not a specialist in programming, and I would be incapable of writing a program, but I know the logic that one must follow to achieve a given result. I know that the instrumental logic and the interpretation of the performer differ from that of the computer, which in itself has no capacity for interpretation. If, for example, one decides that the aleatoric should play a role in the composition of a certain passage, one relies on the willingness and facility of the performer by providing him with a text that he can, following certain rules, manipulate as he pleases; but you provide the computer with a certain amount of

87

statistical data. The performer will have a flexibility of choice that comes from his own familiarity with the music; the computer really chooses in an aleatoric way. The methods are different, but the result in both cases will be very similar.

The problem stems from the fact that one's knowledge of the new technology is not as great as one's knowledge of instrumental music, which is much older.

To break new ground with the computer, one is obliged to check the results, because one does not know exactly what will happen. One has an idea, a circumscribed field of action which points in a certain direction. As for the resulting sound itself, one must test it aurally to be completely sure of it – without that, innovation becomes impossible. On occasions, one is obliged to abandon certain procedures because they do not give the anticipated result; while other procedures, which you hadn't thought of, a priori, turn out to be very interesting and acoustically much more important.

When all is said and done, problems have above all arisen with integrating these phenomena of real time into the interpretation.

Interpretation is a problem that I have been obliged to consider a great deal. In a score that I shall call 'virtual' or 'artificial', there is, strictly speaking, no interpretation. You must modify the data to obtain a change: modify the given intervals, the dynamics, the note values, the aleatoric relationships, etc. You must, in other words, treat digital parameters in a precise fashion. For a musician, information given in a traditional score is more rudimentary and vague than in a digital score, but you can modify it in a more flexible and, above all, more unpredictable way. An accent, for example, while it certainly changes the dynamic, also modifies the note value. Moreover, if the player is in a resonant acoustic, he will 'naturally' play more slowly, just as he will 'naturally' play more quickly in a dry acoustic. The type of acoustic triggers almost involuntary reflexes. The computer does not react to what it hears – perhaps that will come – but it is not the case at the moment. You are obliged to modify, more or less on the spot, according to your experience as a listener. The interpretation, the essential quality of the performer, the ability to make choices, can only exist in the computer in a kind of phantom state.

Composing and performing

Do you think that with changes in real time, one can achieve something more sophisticated than work done on the old magnetic tape?

Infinitely more sophisticated. When you feed into the prism of the technological kaleidoscope the huge variety of which the instrumentalist is capable, it will be multiplied and magnified – something that a fixed magnetic tape is incapable of doing.

In fact, the great thing about real time is that it adds the element of interpretation to electro-acoustical music?

It also adds one more element of uncertainty. On the analogy of Heisenberg's uncertainty principle, no less: the closer you approach an object, the more you submit it to distortions. What is interesting is to take the reality of performance as a concept, as an element which is going to transform the object. A composer like Philippe Manoury knows this very well; he has even applied this problem in a more thorough way than I have done. One takes this uncertainty as an essential part.

One takes it as the fundamental idea and one integrates it into the composition.

Something that I'd like to do eventually is to write a virtual score with variable parameters. Suppose that the instrumentalist played very slowly, suppose that between each signal you had a fairly significant lapse of time – polyphony would be non-existent, time would be distended and the scale of micro-intervals highly restricted. If, on the contrary, the signals given by the instrumentalist were fast and more irregular, the parameters would multiply, the polyphony would grow, the speed would intensify and the intervals expand. What the instrumentalist plays would completely change the nature of the virtual score. I tried to illustrate this mutual influence in the dialogue between two pianos in the second book of my *Structures*, but I have not yet dealt with it with instruments and technology.

That changes fundamentally the basic idea of written music and traditional music.

In traditional Western music, you run successively through all the points of a trajectory that is conceived of and presented as being unique. The 1960s witnessed a great deal of research and innovation concerning open form, but the modifications made to the music itself, which depended on which path you took, were based on fairly simple categories, so that they could be realized immediately. The categories were therefore in contradiction with the complexity of the music itself, which demanded a high level of variability.

Do you think that many composers had this playful side, this wish to short-circuit things?

Yes, there were many of them, even too many. During the sixties, there were certain scores that required numerous pages of explanations, of instructions for use in order to be played, or rather, to be played at! The quality of the result rarely measured up to these multiple rules of the game. The whole thing was turning into a board game.

Like Monopoly ...

Yes. Musical Monopoly. If there is no deep connection between packaging and contents, the result will be of very limited interest: just a sort of Community Chest ...

When you compose this type of score, with these unpredictabilities, how do you manage to resolve the problem of notation?

One has recourse to diagrams: since the exact notation cannot exist, you must avail yourself of a figurative notation. There is nothing new in that! It recalls the old method of notation for the lute: you noted down the action and not the result. In a certain number of scores, that is what I also did. The problem, however, is in the technological tool itself. You either use relatively simple computers with, so to speak, ready-made programs (the risk being that these quickly go out of fashion and are replaced by other computers with different programs which are therefore unusable for the time being); or – and this remains a problem that is also connected to more sophisticated computers – you use more efficient computers which do not change overnight, but whose life is relatively short. It is essential to be able to transfer existing programs on to new computers where, in principle, the results are quicker, but where occasionally new problems are encountered. That, in my opinion, is the greatest handicap that we have to overcome. Compare that with keyboard instruments, whose interface, the keyboard, has not changed for centuries, and you will understand that modernism is not exactly the easiest of existences!

When you consider the early stages with the 4X, which was practically untransportable, you realize now that you can easily move about with a more powerful computer.

There is no longer any problem at all: the size of work tools has been considerably reduced and there is no comparison where reliability is concerned.

How do you view the development there has been in composing with these real-time phenomena in the many years since IRCAM was founded? Do you have the impression that there has been meteoric progress on the scientific level?

Of course there has been progress. I can't say that it's been meteoric, since the day-to-day work doesn't make it look like that. But there has also been a change of attitude, which has eradicated the dogmatism that existed at the outset. There were not many of us at the start: above all, there was Philippe Manoury and myself busy advocating real time; and gradually we were joined by others. When attitudes change, research also changes direction: confidence gradually grows and is consolidated by finished compositions. It is these compositions, and these alone, that will prove the validity of IRCAM, when musical–acoustical– technical coordination will become the basis of new material and thought.

IV

Gestures and the Score

A new vocabulary of gesture

In several of your scores, such as Pli selon pli *or* Éclat, *you were led to conceive a new set of special gestures which permit you to control tempo, dynamics, even the order in which certain sections of the score are played. Did your experience as a conductor influence your ideas as a composer, or was it, on the contrary, your compositional choices that prompted this conception of conducting?*

I began by composing the works, and then found the technique to conduct them. All these sequences, which could appear in any order, these methods of 'breaking up' or 'exploding' the unity of the group and then restoring it – these are the compositional elements that I thought of right at the start. There were also those elements in the score that I modified subsequently, precisely because they were inappropriate, as it was necessary to supply the players with a mountain of explanations before one could begin; and even with these 'directions for use', the risk of error or confusion was out of all proportion to the result.

Who, apart from yourself, can conduct these works?

I am nothing exceptional, I am certainly not a Bodhisattva, furnished with a plethora of arms. Any competent conductor will have no problem in adapting. But to do so, he will need to acquire a different kind of 'vigilance' vis-à-vis the musical context.

You have none the less made conducting an essential part of these scores.

Certainly, and it is a technique that you must know how to acquire, because it is much more linked to the player's gaze and to the geometry of the gesture than the normal, metrical conducting, where everyone follows a unifying gesture. In this latter case, there is no need to give the entries, other than for reasons of security, as it were. You can ensure that you make visual contact with the player or players, without needing a more decisive, a more specific communication. In certain of my works, such as *Rituel in memoriam Maderna*, where you have eight groups of instruments, or *Éclat*, where there are nine instruments, it is absolutely necessary to have a clear picture of the orchestral layout in your mind. If you have to give a precise gesture to a particular instrumentalist in order to have him play a musical cell, you have to make the gesture very precisely in his direction, or else he will not understand that the sign is made specifically for him. The conductor must be able to recall the layout of the players instantly and at all times, all the more so when the events that you wish to create do not happen in a prescribed order, or when this order is improvised and can change at any moment. You must really be able to 'touch' the players, exactly as if they were the keys of a keyboard. To make the wrong gesture can be catastrophic, even with players who have been properly trained in this way of doing things.

You changed the normal orchestral layout in Figures, Doubles, Prismes. *Why?*

I am not fond of changing the usual orchestral layout in the Classical repertoire, because the players are accustomed to the acoustics of sitting in a certain place. Whenever, as a young man, I noticed that musicians were reluctant to adapt to a different layout on stage, I thought that it was a question of laziness. I realize today that there is, beyond the natural inertia of group behaviour, a real problem. Instrumental players are used to hearing each other in a given acoustic, placed either next to certain instruments or far away from them. If you modify this environment, it inevitably takes time – and sometimes a fairly long time – to adapt. In general, therefore, whenever I conduct a new orchestra, I try not to change the position of the players, unless there is some anomaly that really bothers me. Cellos on the inside, violas on the outside, or vice-versa: to change the arrangement has it advantages and its drawbacks, which cancel each other out.

More recently, the nineteenth- and early twentieth-century arrangement has been reintroduced, with the first violins to the conductor's left and the second violins to his right: you can go on arguing about it *ad infinitum*. In certain polyphonic instances, this arrangement has its advantages; in other cases, it contradicts the score. I find that it is ill-advised to be dogmatic on the subject. If there is an arrangement that I do respect without qualification, it is the one adopted in the orchestra pit at Bayreuth, which is the only possible arrangement in that particular design configuration.

The Bayreuth orchestra is arranged in the same way as a symphony orchestra, except that the pit stretches down beneath the stage. There are several ways of arranging the strings of a symphony orchestra – each conductor has his own preference – but when all is said and done, there is not much difference. But at Bayreuth, the strings are arranged in this way: the first violins are placed to the conductor's right, with the sound-holes pointing upwards, and the second violins to the conductor's left, with the sound-holes turned towards the wall, in order that their sonority emerges once it has been reflected and is therefore less brilliant. The violas are placed a level lower; the cellos a level lower still; there are four double basses on either side (the eight double basses are therefore not together), and six harps (grouped on either side with the four double basses). And towards the bottom of the pit you find the woodwind, with eight horns on the right, trumpets and trombones on the left, and at the very bottom the kettledrums and percussion. This arrangement is set in marble; it was invented by Wagner, is sacrosanct and works extremely well. The theatre, moreover, is a piece of sculpture in which the players are placed. According to Wieland Wagner, Karajan tried to place the eight double basses on the same side, but the outcome was not right and he returned to the arrangement invented by Wagner, who knew exactly what he wanted, and I have to say that this arrangement is better.

To return to *Figures, Doubles, Prismes*, the concept of orchestral grouping comes from the idea of a mixture of timbres, which is not the case in a traditional orchestra where you find the four constituent groups – strings, woodwind, brass, percussion – arranged in that order of distance from the conductor, an order which is determined by the acoustic strength of each of these groups, and also by the increase in their importance in the history of orchestral composition.

In Figures, Doubles, Prismes, *the woodwind, brass, strings and percussion are mixed up and dispersed in different orchestral groupings. Was it the first time that you had done that?*

Yes, the first time.

Was this idea linked to what Stockhausen had done in Gruppen?

No, because in *Gruppen* there were three separate orchestras, whereas in my work there is only one orchestra, with groups that are arranged symmetrically: woodwind at the centre, brass on the outside and strings in between, with the percussion placed right at the back. This arrangement is bound up with the idea of stereophony, which was new at the time: the sound is distributed on the platform in a way that is potentially mobile, whereas a Classical orchestra is based on areas of fixed sound. With a genuine mixture of timbres, you can play much more effectively on the relation between sound and space, even on the limited scale of a platform – in other words, in a head-on arrangement. Since *Figures, Doubles, Prismes*, I have greatly expanded this notion of timbre and space by using more flexible arrangements, which are not possible when the orchestra is arranged head-on.

Did this layout already imply the new type of conducting we were talking about?

No. The conducting, in this case, is totally classical. I realized very quickly that one cannot impose 'individual' gestures on an orchestra of a hundred and twenty players: gestures would become far too complicated and the gains would be minimal.

In 1960, I wrote the first version of 'Tombeau', the last movement of *Pli selon pli*, in which groups were to start playing by reacting to '*ad libitum*' gestures from the conductor. It was an immediate catastrophe: the groups lost their place, mistook one gesture for another, and rehearsals did not bring any real improvement. It was the principle that was false, and so I rewrote everything.

These gestures were not, it seems, suited to large ensembles.

The orchestral player requires gestures that are generally simple and directional. If the gestures are too complicated and are made in a sort of abstracted space, as was the case in the first version of 'Don'*, in *Pli selon pli*, there will always be some players who get lost and play at the wrong moment. When I rewrote the piece, I completely sacrificed this idea of freedom. With nine players, on the other hand, as in *Éclat*, the result is infinitely more easy to achieve, and the risk of error becomes almost nonexistent. The individual player is responsible, the connection between conductor and player is much more immediate. In *Sur Incises*, I pitted two ways of conducting against each other in a more systematic manner: what I called 'direction de rassemblement' and 'direction de dispersion'. The result does not really pose any problems.

But in Éclat, *there are some aleatoric sequences in which the players must be constantly 'on guard'. That is something very new. How did they react at the time?*

The first performance of this piece, in Los Angeles in 1965, naturally surprised the players. But they adapted to it, as if

* Actually the second version from 1965, for soprano and orchestra. The first version of 'Don', from 1960, was for soprano and piano. The third and final version also for soprano and orchestra, dates from 1989.

to a game. At any rate, I do not recall any insurmountable difficulties or any great hesitation, as had been the case in the first versions of *Pli selon pli*. That experience had served me well and led me to draw some vital conclusions concerning the score, the instrumental layout and the conductor's gestures.

When you conduct a piece such as Répons *or . . .* explosante-fixe *. . . , you are not placed in the best position to direct the music.*

You are right; one is always in an uncomfortable position to conduct this sort of layout. I therefore requested the help of an assistant who could conduct while I listened to the result in the auditorium – above all, the relationship between the soloists and the loudspeakers, which were positioned around the periphery. There is, by the way, nothing odd about such a layout, which is frequently encountered in opera.

In Répons, *the difficulty comes from the fact that you are situated in the centre and have to conduct soloists who are sometimes a long way away from you, and sometimes even behind you.*

Yes, and there are the same experimental problems in other works: conducting through gesture, and conducting with a strict beat. The same contrast between 'direction de dispersion' and 'direction de rassemblement' is not as systematically simplistic. At any rate, the soloists are conducted for most of the time by gestures that don't relate to tempo, while the orchestra in the centre is for the most part conducted metrically. Metrical conducting can also be applied to the soloists, but in this case the tempo will be inevitably slow, because, with the distance that separates me from the soloists, the beat cannot be too irregular or fast, otherwise the orchestral players will not have time to adapt simultaneously to reading the score and following the conductor.

Individual and collective playing

In Répons, *the six soloists are subject not to your beat but your signals, because they are either too far away or behind you. Only the central orchestra plays 'classically' when you conduct. Do you think that the composer would have had the same ideas if he hadn't also been the conductor?*

I am not sure, but the most important thing stems from the idea of having to compose for a space in which some players are near the centre, and others further away. The consequences of this choice are revealed in the very writing of the score. I thought one could get extremely precise and, in the end, very quick rhythms with players positioned close by, since they have both the score and the conductor in their field of vision. If the players are thirty metres away from the conductor, one cannot ask them to look at their score and the conductor's beat at the same time. That made me think about the way in which one can use the conductor's gesture: it should be infrequent, isolated, specific, indicating the start like a green light for which the player waits. Once this light is on, the soloist has his autonomy, in a field of action parallel to the field of action totally under the control of the central ensemble. All these gestures are precise gestures given to each soloist. That, of course, has consequences, not only as regards gesture, but also for the writing. The free and the fixed dimensions can be superimposed and result in interference patterns. In places, I have calculated the different parts so that the free passages of the soloists roughly correspond to the fixed sequences of the other instruments without being superimposed in a precise manner. That produces a kind of sonic shimmering – like moiré patterns – in relation to a defined context.

That produces rhythmic imbalances . . .

At speed, it can produce an effect that is close to stroboscopic: the central ensemble plays, following the same beat as the soloists without absolute synchronization. In such a juxtaposition, the two beats are so quick that they produce results that are impossible to distinguish from one another. It is now no longer a question of literal accuracy: they give the illusion of being synchronized, because of their speed.

It's a paradoxical situation: one has the impression that all is completely synchronized, but this is not the case.

In effect, the soloists are not really synchronized. It is the conductor, that is to say, myself, who has brought about this acoustical illusion. There are many other circumstances that have allowed me to analyse the mechanisms of perception and how one can play with them. Rehearsals are an inexhaustible source of assistance in this matter. To loosen the link between player and conductor, to make it somehow more inventive – that has been one of my great preoccupations. It may be necessary, as a conductor, constantly to bring the orchestra to heel, but one cannot do that in an infinite variety of ways. What interests me more is to be able to order and throw into disorder, to release and retrieve. In this way, one can obtain an organization of collective time, which becomes individual and then becomes collective once more. These shifting connections within a group, between the collective and the individual, enormously enriches the various dimensions of the music.

And how do you manage to conceive all that from the point of view of writing it down, since you are the one in charge?

You need a method of writing that can be adapted to the aims you are pursuing. Today, of course, I have much more experience than previously; I know that if I write irregular note values according to different subdivisions, specific changes or flexibilities in tempo, the instrumental players will be forced to assume an individuality, an independence vis-à-vis my gesture. In *Sur Incises*, there are certain moments of great flexibility between the pianists and the conductor. But I must also mention another dimension: the acoustics. Whenever one deals with resonating instruments,* the notion of time is complicated by a phenomenon that is quite independent of control – a phenomenon which concerns the richness and the length of resonance. That is also going to interfere with the conductor's direction, and cannot be precisely notated. It is up to the players to react individually to this acoustical property of their instrument.

Is there a sense in which you compel the players to take charge themselves?

Completely! As Stockhausen did in the 1950s with his *Zeit-masse*. I pay tribute to him. That was for me a great experience. When he wrote *Zeitmasse*, I had already composed

---

* Boulez is referring to such instruments as piano, harp, celesta, glockenspiel and vibraphone – all of which are plucked or struck and can then be left to resonate.

Le Marteau sans maître, where there are a number of passages with very flexible tempo, which is constantly fluctuating, now fixed, now fluid: in that way, I managed to enrich the notion of tempo through an extreme mobility, continuous or discontinuous. This tempo, however, applied to the whole group, while in *Zeitmasse* there were moments when the five instruments became independent of each other. The superimposing of constant or variable speeds (*accelerando* or *ritardando*) is fairly difficult to realize in a fixed tempo, moving from one given metronomic speed to another. Personally, I tend to trust the musical content, unless the relationship between tempi is explicit, as it is in certain works by Stravinsky or Carter. Pulsation, or its absence, is what makes us react to a musical idea. There is an infinite variety of ways of using musical pulse – whether it be very slow or very fast, regular or irregular – but these means are always the products of conscious decisions. The absence of pulse, on the other hand, depends on phenomena of which we are not totally in control, acoustics being the most important, but also the interference between different actions, different ways of playing, the fact that a preparation of an instrument (a silent piano, for example) prevents the player from maintaining an underlying pulse, as no sound results.

With . . . explosante-fixe *. . . , you seemed to return to a quite different style of writing.*

The writing is designed for a homogenous group, placed facing the audience.

As for a traditional theatre?

For a traditional theatre or stage; the music spreads from the stage to the auditorium, transforming the sound of the solo flute. There are not, therefore, any special problems in this work as far as conducting is concerned. What concerns me more is the diffusion of sound, that is to say the computer, the mixing desk and the loudspeakers. The trickiest problem is always the loudspeakers.

You mean spatialization . . .

Of course, but also sound quality and above all the anonymity of loudspeakers. It's true that a loudspeaker cannot be considered in the same terms as an instrument such as the violin, which has its own acoustical quality and brilliance. What I fear most in loudspeakers is, in fact, anonymity, levelling out. That reminds me of a theatrical experience I've occasionally described. In London, during the 1970s, I saw a play directed by Peter Brook. During the first half, the actors delivered their text straight, which was therefore easy to understand. But in the second half, the actors were miked, which made it very difficult to know who was speaking, since the voices did not only come from where the actors stood; the sounds were lost in an aura of loudspeaker noise which came from every direction.

Was it very unsettling?

It was extraordinary to experience this pulverizing of sound through the levelling out of each voice and its spatial placing. During the first rehearsals of *Répons*, there were passages where there was no transformation of the piano, the harp, etc., and other moments where the sound was transformed. The difference was unbearable: listening to the live instruments was in complete contradiction with the transformed sounds diffused through the loudspeakers. We were faced with an impossible mixture of conflicting sounds, to the extent that, even for passages where the sound was not transformed, we also diffused the instrumental sound through loudspeakers in order to obtain consistency between original and transformed sounds.

That would tend to prove that the acoustical quality of loudspeakers has not developed as much as the rest of technology.

They are technologically very advanced, but they are completely anonymous; they have neither colour nor variation of response. The definition of a good loudspeaker is to be equally responsive over the largest possible register – whereas, in my view, the qualities of loudspeakers ought to be very different. But perhaps I'm mistaken and my views are distorted by instrumental practice.

Where to place the loudspeakers is often equally problematical in Répons, *because the person who, for example, finds himself sitting next to the cimbalon loudspeaker hears virtually nothing but the cimbalon. Isn't the solution, when all is said and done, to perform in a large hall where all the loudspeakers are at an acceptable distance from the audience?*

In Los Angeles, we performed *Répons* in a very large gymnasium. It was difficult to conduct because the soloists were so far away, but the audience heard the music more globally, since they were sitting sufficiently far away from all the sound sources. One cannot, however, say that there is an ideal listening space where all sounds can be heard equally.

With each orchestral layout, members of the audience will hear an unbalanced sound, depending on whether they are distant or close to certain instruments or loudspeakers.

Illusions and kaleidoscopes

In ... explosante-fixe *..., you tried in particular to develop instrumental transformations of sound.*

Yes, it's a kind of puzzle, with musical segments that alternate more or less rapidly and in a more or less predictable manner. I think you can recognize easily enough the constituent elements, but they always come in an order that is difficult, if not impossible, to anticipate. In 'Transitoire VII', the manner in which the elements occurred was deliberately abrupt. In 'Transitoire V', I ensured that there was always a sort of transition between two elements.

You attempt to short-circuit perception.

Perception is both assured by the elements that it recognizes thanks to their position in the ensemble, their 'envelope', and deceived, because it never knows when, precisely, to expect this recognition. For me, it is always more surprising to open out on two simultaneous levels: one where you are safe, the other where you are in doubt. This dialectic of safety and doubt is, in my opinion, one of the most interesting elements in our perception of music.

Is recognition made at the level of instrumental timbre?

Each segment is linked to a timbre, a register, a density, an instrumental colour, etc.; the reference is always very precise, even if the presentation varies. But at the moment when this segment reappears, it cannot be anticipated mechanically. It's a sort of 'scanning' of layers of similar cells, based on the same characteristics, from the simplest and shortest to the longest and most complex. The form then consists of sweeping these layers from the ensemble by following certain fairly flexible directions. The form then establishes itself, reveals itself, as the constituent elements of each layer dwindle. In 'Transitoire VII', the changes from segment to segment are abrupt, which implies instantaneous changes of tempo that the conductor must react to without hesitation.

Were you trying to modify your own habits as a conductor?

It did not give me much trouble, because I thought the work through like that, and I perform it like that. There are works that have caused me much greater problems, like certain passages in *Répons,* or the end of *Éclat/Multiples* which is extremely difficult, less on the level of gesture than in the alternation of rapid groups in free time, of unequal length, with bars written in a slow tempo, precisely defined. That is really difficult to think through.

Do you mean it's difficult to think through or to put across?

For the conductor, it's difficult at first to think through, then to put across. The conducting must change instantly from the rapid groups to slow groups, and, for rapid groups, it is necessary to give a variable beat, according to their length. It's equally difficult for the players, for they have no time to think. If the conductor changes speed, changes beat, the players must instantly change with him. It's not just a question of working method, it's also a question of acquiring a common instinct. The musicians must be completely relaxed, so that you do not feel the slightest hesitation when there is a change of speed. It's like the technique of *trompe-l'œil* in sixteenth-century homes, where the artist tries to make you confuse sky and ceiling. I have often used this comparison: put a candle inside a kaleidoscope and you will get a multitude of candles. A real object is enough to engender a multitude of virtual objects; the barrier dissolves between categories which, initially, seemed totally incompatible.

The rewritten works

You very often rewrite your pieces. Does this involve making substantial changes to the original musical text?

It's always a question of deepening the text. Of course, I correct what to me appears inadequate – but that rarely comes about because what I have written is clumsy or wrong, but because the thought and its realization are insufficient.

This wish to revise your scores also stems from the fact that you can test them personally in your capacity as conductor.

Almost always when a difficulty in the score proves itself to be insurmountable, it's because there is an error both in its conception and its notation. You cannot always blame the inadequacy of the players. So you have to correct the score, not to make it easier, but more effective – I repeat, effective. I prefer a definitive text which lends itself to an almost perfect realization – an absolute is attained only rarely – to a text that can only succeed through happy chance . . . Of course, my experience as an orchestral conductor has helped me to discover the best performing conditions, but even if I had not been my own interpreter, I should have reacted in the same way.

Visage nuptial *is a case in point?*

It's a work that I am fond of and which has been rewritten several times. The first version was composed in 1946, a long time ago! It was written for solo voice and a very small ensemble, and scored for two ondes martenot, piano and percussion. With hindsight, I became aware of the limitations of the ondes martenot for my musical project, whereas in 1945–6 I had been attracted by several possibilities of this electronic instrument, such as intervals, registers and timbres. Later, between 1952 and 1953, I found that the solo voice did not convey the breadth I wished to give to René Char's poem. I therefore decided on two solo voices, soprano and alto, and a chorus of female voices, which meant using a large orchestra, which corresponded to the volume of the sung sound. At this period, I indulged myself in extremely Utopian orchestration, using the notion of 'Klangfarbenmelodie' pushed to the limit: all in a highly theoretical spirit, connected to my style of writing of this period, which was rather ascetic and very rigorous. I would add that at that time I had no direct experience of orchestration.* As a result, although the choral writing might have worked fairly well, the orchestral writing failed to achieve what I was aiming for.

You used quarter-tones in the score.

Yes, but I omitted them in the most recent version, because I quickly saw that when you write these quarter-tones for

---

* By 1952–3, two large instrumental or orchestral works of Boulez had been performed: *Polyphonie X* (1949–50) was played at the 1951 Donaueschingen Festival, conducted by Hans Rosbaud; *Le soleil des eaux* (1948–50) had been played in its first version for solo voices and small orchestra in Paris in 1950, conducted by Roger Désormière. Due to his commitments as conductor of incidental music at the Théâtre Jean-Louis Barrault, Boulez missed both performances and had to rely on tapes alone to judge his orchestration. Hence his statement here that he had 'no direct experience' of orchestration.

the violin section of an orchestra, for example, the players can only be very approximate, above all in the upper register – because group accuracy, which is difficult enough with the simple semitone, becomes entirely hypothetical when it's a question of smaller intervals. There were other performing difficulties, more specifically rhythmic. At the outset, I thought that this was in large measure due to my conducting, because in 1957, when the work was premièred, I was far from being very skilled! When, in 1977–8, I was asked once more to conduct this work, I told myself that with the conducting experience I had acquired, I ought to see what I could salvage. But after the first rehearsal, I cancelled the performance and decided to rewrite the work from start to finish. I wanted to rediscover the 'flesh' that this work had had in 1946 and which I had 'desiccated' in 1952 with too much that was theoretical: I therefore rethought the whole score. But you can follow almost note for note the process of transformation in the three versions: the form has remained the same, things have remained unchanged, the content has remained identical, but the writing is much more detailed, especially in the third movement. There were, of course, moments when I doubted if I could rediscover the old trail – I wanted to preserve it as the essence of the work.

What happened to the quarter-tones?

In their place I substituted a dense polyphony of small intervals, thanks to the multiplication of voices overlapping each other, but in semitones. With this type of writing, which was much more detailed, I achieved something that made up for the quarter-tones of 1946.

Have you ever altered a score – I'm thinking of Répons *– during rehearsals?*

Yes. When, for example, there is a difference between the rehearsal space and the performing space. The acoustics do not sound at all the same in a studio of 50 m² as in a hall of 2 000 m². That calls into question definitions of speed, spatialization or dynamics, although, on the whole, the musical substance remains the same. From this point of view, it is important to be able not only to rehearse but also to complete the work in a large space, since this space plays a role not only in the conception but also in putting the finishing touches to the work.

As far as sound diffusion and placing the loudspeakers is concerned, there are still serious problems, since there are not enough 'good places' in traditional halls. You are often seated closer to one loudspeaker than another.

Traditional halls are quite simply inadequate. That was the reason why I was keen to have an auditorium constructed at La Villette which was truly convertible, and also why *Répons* has always been played in 'empty' places, without any structure in the way, in order to place those players who have not been electronically transformed in the centre of the playing area, with the audience seated around this group and the players who have been electronically transformed placed behind and around the audience – with the loudspeakers increasing this sensation of space around the audience. That would be impossible in a traditional hall, with the exception of the Boston Symphony Hall, where seats can be removed from the stalls to create a totally open space. For me, the hall of the future could well be one in which the equipment was not necessarily extravagantly expensive but movable, and could be arranged in a great variety of ways. The more clumsily sophisticated a hall is, if I can put it like that, the less it is usable and accessible. In general, greater attention should be paid to good acoustics than to the equipment.

. . . explosante-fixe . . . *is also a piece that has often been re-worked . . .*

That is a very different case. In . . . *explosante-fixe* . . . , I gradually developed an idea which has changed completely from its original conception. In the first version for ensemble, there were seven independent sections for eight instruments, the seventh voice being played in heterophony by two instruments. At the beginning, each voice remains strictly in its own register, which explains, in part, the title. Instruments were supposed to interact, by means of electronic connections, projecting themselves on each other. The connections proved to be too complex to work effectively; the same level of complexity from one voice to another produced results that were pretty unpredictable and hardly perceptible. I then abandoned this initial project, and isolated the role of the flute by revising its part. I then intended to realize two versions: one for flute and electronics and the other for flute and ensemble, but I was afraid that this would become too demonstrative and didactic. I finally put these two opposing versions into different sections of the same work: in 'Transitoire VII', therefore, the virtual score competing with the group is very important, while in 'Transitoire V' it is the transformations of the flute that predominate.

Multiple images

Listening to . . . explosante-fixe *. . . , one is struck by a pro-liferation of timbres and textures. Is it not true that, when all is said and done, this multiplication of images comes from your involvement with certain pieces from the tradi-tional repertoire?*

Certainly. The two composers who have most influenced me in recent years are Wagner and Mahler. Not, of course, their style, but their use of the orchestra. Today, I find that, even in works that I love, like those of Debussy and Ravel, the orchestra is used in a relatively simple and very straight-forward way, which I certainly do not consider to be a fault. In Debussy's *Jeux,* the orchestra is conceived of more as a mass. Mahler's thought, however, is organized accord-ing to a very different pattern. That encouraged me to use the resources of the orchestra in a way that was sometimes extremely differentiated. In my *Notations,* I used the idea, which derives from Wagner, of an orchestration seen as a phenomenon of acoustical illusion. What I often seek is not one image but the superimposition of several images. It is in this direction of generalized ambiguity, by the way, that the orchestra has evolved. In the baroque era, there were spe-cific combinations which were used, for example, for this or that piece, such as one finds in the *Cantatas,* the *Passions* or the *Christmas Oratorio* of Bach. With Bach, there is already a sort of superimposing of instrumental images, such as at the beginning of the 'Sanctus' of the *B minor Mass.* The truth is that the nearer you get to the modern orchestra, the more it is the case that the individual instrument is merely a moment, one possibility of instrumentation in contrast to a partial or total tension of all the available timbres. Berlioz already used this contrast in a striking way, especially in the works from the first half of his career when he was not yet aiming for the classicism of Gluck. The closer one gets to the twentieth century, first with Wagner, then Richard Strauss, the more one approaches an orchestral writing of illusion, of acoustical perspective. Later on, the same substratum, from the point of view of the idea, is transcribed differently – something that you find in early Stravinsky. More recently still, a single, main-line principal voice is 'acoustically' deflected around the instruments according to different trajectories: in this way, it's possible to renew certain techniques that had become academic. I no longer write canons as they were practised in baroque music, but I write derivative lines which correspond, in a way, to a principle of acoustical echo, and which are no longer heard as canonic imitations in the strict sense. In *Le Visage nuptial* and in *Notations*, I have made great use of this technique of acoustical derivative lines, which are distorted projections of a principal melodic line.

Isn't Notations *a different case, because it's an orchestral reworking of little piano pieces? Liszt's* Paraphrases *spring to mind . . .*

No, because we are not dealing with paraphrases or adaptations, as with Liszt. Rather belatedly – about thirty years later – I took the original text as a seed, as it were, in order to develop ideas, from which I could now see that you could derive many more possibilities than I had done in

1945, when I composed the original version for piano. The form was bound to grow, since one cannot ask an orchestra to play little pieces lasting several seconds and based on a single idea. That would not only be illogical, but quite simply out of the question, and out of proportion . . .

V

Conducting and Teaching

Transmitting knowledge

It seems that you have taught orchestral conducting more often than composition. Is this through personal choice, or is there in orchestral conducting something more concrete to teach?

I think that conducting, like all interpretative art indeed, is easier to teach than composition. As far as composition is concerned, you can teach someone to write and hear music, but it is really through analysis that composition is taught. And that is what I did when I gave a course at Basle for three consecutive years. As for conducting an orchestra, it is in fact easier to teach certain technical principles, certain gestures by referring to a given text. One can equally learn how to anticipate the entry of an instrument, how to conduct difficult rhythms or how to find one's way about a score in which there are no traditional beat-patterns. Personally, I learned all these principles by myself, face to face with the players. I probably had a certain gift for that, which permitted me to put things right as we went along – one can, in effect, teach these technical principles – but beyond that, one must also analyse the score to sift out what is important. The further you get in the art of interpretation, the more you realize that there are things which can be established, if not very quickly, at least with a minimum of work, while other things are more difficult and require work and rehearsal – not necessarily to do with rhythmic matters, but the balance of sound, the element of continuity, particularly in contemporary music, where the phrasing is not always automatically understood. These are things that must be insisted on. With conducting, it's above all a matter of knowing the score that enables you to find the appropriate gesture to guarantee the best performance of the work.

A gesture that one must, in the final analysis, find oneself.

Exactly. To imitate the gestures of other conductors is completely useless, since it's a question of length of arm, suppleness of hands, technique with or without a baton, of physiognomy even. These are purely individual matters. The important thing is that there is a connection between what one knows of the score, what one wishes to hear and the gesture which will produce this.

Do you not convey your own interpretation in a conducting course?

Certainly, I cannot do otherwise, even if we're dealing with the Classical or Romantic repertoire. 'This is how *I* do it. Now make me understand what you want by making a suitable gesture. Let your gesture really correspond to what you want to hear.' I often say that to those who imitate me because they have seen and heard that it works. If I conduct a workshop on Debussy's *Jeux*, the student will certainly have to find a certain precision in the fluidity, whereas in *The Rite of Spring* this fluidity would be completely superfluous: what is needed here is a definite strictness, with, however, a suggestion of phrasing. A gesture must be found that is both strict and precise and can convey subdivisions to the players or the absence or even the irregularity of the subdivisions. For that, you certainly need a minimum of technique, so that the players can fully understand where they are within the beats. It's what I call the geometry of the gesture. In difficult works, it must not be forgotten that the players will not always be looking at the conductor. They will need to look at their part, even if they know it well. It is important, therefore, at the moment you look at them, that they are sure of the gesture you have made. These principles can be learned, but if you gesture mechanically, it will be useless.

What are the qualities and the faults that you notice immediately when you work with a young conductor?

The first fault you notice is that the conductor is so preoccupied with himself that he doesn't hear what is happening – conducting is not just a question of giving initiatives but also of being receptive to what the orchestra does. If there is not this reciprocity, a conductor will fail. You notice immediately those who conduct mechanically 'for themselves' and who are not receptive to what they hear. The second thing that you notice, even with those conductors who have passed the beginner's stage, is the quality of what they hear. Can they hear intervals and – this is essential – can they hear mistakes? One must, after all, be able not only to adjust the quality of the sound perceived but also to balance the chords in which each note is played by an instrument from a different family which, moreover, may be situated at varying degrees of distance from the conductor. This sort of writing can be found in the works of Webern and even Berg and Schoenberg. When that is the case, the players who are seated too far from one another cannot hear each other, and it's up to the conductor to solve the problems of intonation and balance. It's sometimes very difficult, because certain chords are very chromatic, and the conductor must be very quick to notice which players are not well in tune. In such a case, I teach them to break down the chord into its different key constituents, because it is easier to hear like that. Once the problems of intonation have been solved, you can superimpose these different constituents. From this moment on, the players know what to look out for in order to 'tune a chord', just as one speaks of 'tuning a piano'. These are complex things to learn, because they require not only an ability to hear well, but also to take initiatives and analyse problems.

How many times have you given seminars on orchestral conducting?

I twice gave courses after the composition classes at Basle in 1965 and 1969. Both lasted three weeks, with a repertoire that consisted of *The Rite of Spring*, Berg's Op. 6 and *Violin Concerto*, Schoenberg's *Erwartung* and Webern's *Variations for Orchestra*. Although not easy to conduct, these are fundamental works of the twentieth-century repertoire. Also on the programme were a work by Stockhausen and *Le Marteau sans maître*. Each day, there was a rehearsal in the morning, preparation time in the afternoon and another rehearsal in the evening. At the end of these three weeks, there were conducted concerts, which is essential for injecting a certain tension into the orchestra and making sure that the course was not a mere exercise.

What other experiences have you had in this field?

I have not given many courses on conducting: one with the London Symphony Orchestra, one with the Cleveland

Orchestra at Carnegie Hall and one with the EIC at the Centre Acanthes in Villeneuve-lès-Avignon in 1988. I began conducting the LSO in the 1967–8 season, and made recordings with them, particularly Berlioz and Mahler. But when I was asked to become Musical Director of the BBC, I no longer conducted other orchestras – which is absolutely normal. Having freed myself from my obligations to the BBC, I began to give concerts again, especially with the LSO, and in 1995 and 2000 I toured with this orchestra, giving concerts which featured my own works, those by composers who had most influenced me and those of a younger generation. The rare times that I have given conducting courses, or rather seminars, it was with the LSO and the Cleveland Orchestra, but with only two sessions, that is very expensive. With the LSO, I held a single session of three hours in both 1995 and 2000 on one of my pieces I was working on, but these were not in-depth studies. The students were all studying conducting, they were true apprentices, and I gave them Schoenberg's Piano Concerto to work on. With the Cleveland Orchestra, on the other hand, both at Carnegie Hall and the Cité de la Musique in Paris, I was dealing with young professionals who had been selected on merit, real musicians who knew their profession, even if they hadn't much experience. It's for this reason that I chose Debussy's *Jeux* and Messiaen's *Chronochromie*. At Halifax, in 1991, I encountered only one candidate who was very gifted – George Pehlivanian. He's now making a career for himself and conducts in Holland. It has to be said that, in the field of contemporary music, the conductors who come forward have no training, which is not their fault, since the academies and the conservatoires offer only a very weak and often mediocre education in this area – by which I mean the twentieth century in general.

You none the less seem more interested in teaching con-
ducting than composition. In fact, in your life as a com-
poser, you have successfully avoided teaching composition.

I think that composition *per se* cannot be taught, except by
analysing scores, where you can point things out. But basi-
cally, I do not have a teacher's soul. I like teaching in small
rations but I would be incapable of being a teacher
throughout the year. Two or three days a year of short,
intense work are enough for me, because I think that the
students should be given shock treatment in respect of high
standards. Those students who are at this standard will be
on a high, those who are not will very probably go under.
It's really like playing double or quits! From this point of
view, I am very 'Darwinian'. I think it is utterly useless
dragging a weight behind you which you know perfectly
well will not reach the top of the hill. I expect only limited
progress to be made in this time with students of a very
high standard. I've also had experience of young orchestras, teaching them interpretation through conducting
them myself – at the Cité de la Musique at La Villette for a
week, no more, during the summer of 1995.

You have none the less launched an educational project at
the Cité de la Musique. You don't seem to be so uninter-
ested in education!

That was something important, for there are not sufficient
links between the teaching of composition and the teaching
of interpretation. How do you expect someone to analyse a
work if he is not present at a rehearsal where it is thoroughly discussed? Teachers of composition and conducting
ought to be in the same boat – and that is unfortunately not

the case at the moment, which I find disastrous. Instead, the score is analysed in a composition class, one observes the combination of oboe and cello, and one finds it very beautiful. But what does that mean, 'very beautiful'? It's only because one teaches that it is 'very beautiful'. One then proceeds to combine oboe and cello, as in Stravinsky. But if one does not know why three solo cellos and three oboes combine so beautifully, as for example in the *Symphony of Psalms*, it is pointless. All you are doing is observing what's there. What is necessary is to hear these instruments separately and show that if the cellos use a lot of vibrato, the combination will suddenly become horrific. That is what composers should be taught to understand, not just that oboes and cellos go very well together, but also the conditions of such a marriage. A conductor with great experience needs to spend time with a teacher of composition in order to prepare such a rehearsal. That, of course, assumes a great deal of availability and devotion. This type of teaching ought to be essential, for one cannot constantly separate the writing from the practice, as is generally the case.

You opened a teaching course at the Cité de la Musique with a class on the interpretation of twentieth-century music. What were your objectives?

The principal aim was to give a concert at the end of the course, because to teach without subjecting your work to the public is to remove a certain tension from the performance. I chose a programme that would involve a lot of players and provide a balance of different styles: Schoenberg's *Chamber Symphony* Op. 9, which, in a certain sense, belongs to the German post-Romantic style with a tradition that is fairly difficult to assimilate with regard to both the balance and the notes; Varèse's *Déserts*, with its monolithic blocks of brass and wind, since there are no strings; a piece from . . . *explosante-fixe* . . . , which is easier to perform but which introduces the audience to a specific style; and Carter's *Penthode*, the most difficult work from many points of view and rarely played. Quite an overview. David Robertson was also involved with Stravinsky's *Symphonies for wind instruments*, and there was a piece by Varèse, Donatoni's *Cadeau* and Peter Eötvös's *Chinese Opera*, which sets out a different form of rhythmic notation. There was, in other words, an enormous range of twentieth-century music, from the classics to the most recent works. It was a good experience, even if the recruitment of students could have been improved. There was, however, a good sense of cohesion between the musicians of different countries. But that's not to say that interpretation is becoming internationalized, for there are still schools. When the French tackle Schoenberg, for example, they play *sforzati* in the same way as they play them in Stravinsky – that is to say, fairly brutally – whereas the Germans play *sforzati* almost after the beat: the result is something that is longer, more supple and more weighty. These are notions of style that must be learned when one performs the music of the twentieth century. Such works are not very well known stylistically, and this gap in education should at all costs be remedied. The twentieth-century repertoire is much too rarely played, which is one of the reasons why such hostility is sometimes shown to contemporary music. How many times are pieces like Schoenberg's Op. 16 performed in a season? Practically never. That is also to do with conductors who often play the same repertoire. I find it deplorable that for many of them the repertoire ends with Mahler. Thirty years ago, no one knew Mahler!

This educational project, then, filled a gap. How do you intend developing it?

This project is a fundamental aspect of La Villette. I don't know if the conservatoires have enough time to prepare for such a project. It's true that the music of the twentieth century demands technical abilities that are beyond a beginner. This repertoire would need to be tackled at the end of a student's studies. But does a student at the end of his studies have the time to devote himself to the Second Viennese School, to Stravinsky or Bartók? Parallel to that, of course, he would also need to know the repertoire of the past. If one has never played any Wagner, it will be difficult. But has a conservatoire orchestra ever played an opera by Wagner?

You are asking for a huge amount of knowledge which students could only acquire if they have limitless time at their disposal.

I would find it normal for conservatoire students to play if not an act, then at least a large scene of Wagner. One must learn how to play Wagner's operas. After all, one learns the symphonic repertoire from Beethoven and Brahms up to Mahler. But it is also necessary to know the repertoire that is not solely symphonic – the operas of Mozart, for example. As a rule, musicians beginning a professional career have to learn as they go along. But students at the Juilliard School mount operas which are not so easy. And they certainly put on the Italian repertoire – it's important for their training.

Yet you approached the contemporary repertoire before the Classical!

I am the exception who confirms the rule. I learned everything as I went along, but if at that time I had been interested in, or attracted by, classes at the conservatoire, I would have attended them. The teachers of conducting and composition were of little interest when I was a student at the conservatoire. As a student, I already had very precise ideas on what a teacher ought to be. I had followed Messiaen's harmony class, but the other classes were totally inadequate.

You are not keen on becoming too involved in teaching, but on the other hand you recognize that someone who is self-taught can waste a lot of time.

One can develop later. Education is no panacea, either. I mean that it never supplies talent to those who have none; it can simply nourish talent. In any case, music is not only made by geniuses but, at a certain level, by people who are professionally quite capable of fulfilling their function. There are different levels and it's absolutely normal to encourage those who wish to climb to the highest levels. Education has its limits. It's not a question of time. You give an impulse to someone who wishes to make quicker progress than others, to someone you see more frequently and who you will be able to help develop. That is very obvious with certain teachers who were very average in their professional life and who were very good teachers. On a different level, Schoenberg taught composition for forty years and only had two exceptional pupils – right at the start of his career. He then had pupils who were of a reasonable standard, but certainly none who were comparable to Berg and Webern. Perhaps it's a question of genes, but I can only note the fact. On the other hand, what remains of

Messiaen's very adventurous students from 1944 to 1945?

That has nothing to do with the teacher, nor the circumstances, for Messiaen's classes at that period were held outside the conservatoire, off the beaten track, and did not lead to a diploma; they were held 'for the beauty of the thing'. But that did not make a genius of those who were not geniuses. That is the reason why I am sceptical about teaching; I am quite ready to take it on if necessary, but I know very well that it has its limits. Teaching is only a beginning; it is teaching yourself that is important. I have often said it and I still think it: I much prefer those who chose to teach themselves to those who ended up teaching themselves by chance. You can develop this wish with someone who, later, might 'hit you in the face'. That is perfect. He must also kill the father.

When you look at a work like Penser la musique aujourd'hui, *isn't that, in a way, teaching from a distance? How do you view this work today?*

It's a way of making others think, that is all I ask. It is not teaching in the traditional sense of the term. I say: 'This is what I have done, this is what others have done: find your way through that.' I ask for neither support nor a purely positive reaction. Reaction is what is required. So much the better if the reaction is positive; likewise if it is negative. I am a bad father. I am like Jean-Jacques Rousseau: if I had had children, I would have put them in care, so that they might grow up by themselves. The idea of this work was, in a certain way, to take stock of the techniques of composition in the 1960s. That is the reason why I have never attempted to revise it. It's an inventory. It has no other claim. It was, in effect, the result of those courses that I was giving at Darmstadt. I had been asked to publish them. I wrote them down in full. Two or three volumes were planned, but in the end I only wrote one because I found it was sufficient. The books that I published later are not written in such a systematic way. Perhaps I found all that useless, and then my life as a performer took up a lot of time . . .

The willing autodidact

If one wanted to assess your double activity as composer and conductor, could one say that, as a composer, you were enriched by your conducting?

Yes. I shall tell you why. When I was a student at the Paris Conservatoire, I learned neither conducting nor orchestration. Olivier Messiaen was at this time my professor of harmony, but outside the conservatoire he would occasionally give lessons in analysis that were extremely productive. However, I have to admit that he wasn't enormously interested in orchestration, despite his practical experience and know-how; rhythm and melody fired his imagination much more. Even when he analysed Ravel or Stravinsky's *Petrushka*, as I recall on two occasions, he was not very fond of discussing timbre. Above all, I learned from scores and treatises. But it was Roger Désormière who inspired me most in this area. I'm not just talking about the practical side of conducting, but also the practical knowledge of orchestration. During my frequent visits to his rehearsals, I used to read the scores and notice what was interesting about the timbre in the various instrumental combinations. I recall, amongst others, his rehearsals of the *Chant du rossignol* and how I listened with great profit to the way he explained and clarified this or that passage of the score.

The best way would be therefore to follow rehearsals rather than read treatises.

You must read them as well in order to learn how instruments function, and also to become aware of their tessitura and potential. Berlioz's treatise reveals, above all, much about his thought, but there is an enormous difference between this past and our present. Well after I had finished my studies, I read Rimsky-Korsakov's treaty on orchestration, which is, on topics such as balance and the instrumentation of chords, extremely practical. It is not at all surprising that Stravinsky got off to such a brilliant start, for Rimsky-Korsakov had been his teacher. As for me, I partly missed out on this education. At the time when I was at the conservatoire – from 1943 to 1948 – there were virtually no teachers of composition, and that is no exaggeration. Officially, Messiaen taught harmony; unofficially, he taught analysis. I learned much with him about musical lanaguage and harmony, but much less about orchestration. And so it is true that the practical experience I gained from conducting taught me a vast amount and enriched my knowledge of composition.

Do you mean that conducting influenced your way of conceiving music?

It made me more critical vis-à-vis the connection between theoretical speculation and practical realization. I have always been in favour of theoretical speculation, for it is that which carries you forward. If you remain restricted by performance, you will never achieve anything. I should never have been able to write *Répons* if I had not thought in those terms. Invention is the wellspring, all the gestures and processes are a consequence of it. My first concern is to create something, and only afterwards find the means to realize it. But there are often things that arise from the act of conducting. To start with, I now follow a rationale to which I am much more attentive than before. Practical experience tells me almost by instinct that if something is only 40 per cent possible to bring off, it is better to write more simply. But I had already thought much about these things in the 1960s. When I wrote the first book of *Structures pour deux pianos*, which is in itself a complex enough work, there was an earlier version that was rhythmically completely unperformable. There were divisions of seventeen notes in the time of fifteen which were totally theoretical, and, as a pianist, I realized immediately that it could not be played with any precision.

Whenever I played my own works on the piano, and even more so when I conducted them, I thought fairly early on about the sort of 'result' that would be effective. For when one composes in too complex a manner, the performer inevitably simplifies. Whereas if one writes in a different way, asking, for example, for these fifteen or seventeen notes to be played between one downbeat and the next, the result is much securer. That produces a much more interesting performance than would have been the case if the performers had been obliged to simplify something that had been written in too complicated a fashion. It makes you aware of the difference between your imagining and its realization. Another consequence of performing is the importance attached to discovering points of reference in musical form. If a structure is very complex and develops at a certain moment, it must be indicated. In . . . *explosante-fixe* . . . , for example, the structure is very complex, because it is a puzzle in which each part of the puzzle has a register of its own and one follows the trajectory (even if it is difficult to follow), because there is always a formal element which returns, and you hear it despite yourself. If the reflex is that Pavlovian, this structure is perceptible. I think that what conducting an orchestra has taught me is this: the more complex the structure, the more you must link it to a simple parameter. It is one of the permanent features with Wagner; if the leitmotivs recur in a very obvious form, it is to put you back on track when you have lost your way in the structure. The structure of Wagner's operas is at times excessively complex, and it is thanks to the leitmotivs that one can get one's bearings in an act that lasts two hours.

Conducting has therefore provided you, the composer, with a practical side.

It has caused me to reflect on speculation and performance. They are like two mirrors. You have the mirror of speculation and the mirror of performance, which reflect each other. That is indispensable.

Every composer, therefore, ought to have the experience of conducting an orchestra?

When a composer is involved in rehearsing one of his works, he ought to be capable of this double role. There are composers who have had their works played throughout their life and have made not the slightest progress in this area. As a consequence, I find it very difficult to take them seriously. As much as I can admire certain ideas, I find that their inventiveness fails to come across in performance. A work is not pure invention, it requires to be performed. Otherwise, it is incomplete.

Do you think that, as far creativity is concerned, the practical side can sometimes prevail over the creative side?

No, because if one creates, one creates in the abstract, and it's only afterwards that you see how the practical side feeds the imagination. Realism, as a phenomenon, does not cut out invention, but pushes it in the right direction so that your reflexes become quicker.

Today, you conduct some of the most prestigious orchestras, those from Chicago, Cleveland, Berlin and Vienna. How would you define the special qualities of these orchestras?

Firstly, each player has a complete mastery of his or her instrument. They are orchestral virtuosi. The second quality comes from the fact that these musicians are intelligent players who understand quickly what the conductor wants. They can carry out his wishes almost immediately. The third and final quality is their sense of ensemble. This is crucial, to give each section both a homogenous style and colour.

Is it a question of individual personal commitment?

Their training predisposes them to merge their individual qualities into a collective harmony. The orchestras that I most often like to conduct possess both homogeneity and brilliance; their individual qualities blend into a collective quality. Although it is true that players from different countries possess different instrumental techniques, that is not, to my ears, a crucial or, at any rate, an intractable factor in the diversity of orchestral sounds. Orchestral training in France was for a long time neglected, and that has hindered the development of a collective cohesion. That has greatly changed in recent decades, but work still remains to be done for their habits to be radically changed; there is certainly goodwill, but the effort sustained over many years must now be continued. When I founded the Ensemble InterContemporain, I very much had in mind Georg Szell and the Cleveland Orchestra, which he had the patience and persistence to form over more than twenty years. The first concerts of the Ensemble were sometimes difficult, but after twenty-five years of existence, a cohesion and, yes, a virtuosity have been achieved which the works demand.

Do you no longer intend to conduct orchestras that are not of this quality?

I try to maintain a steady relationship with those orchestras to which I am connected, instead of conducting here, there and everywhere without any real artistic aim. And it is, of course, more satisfying if all the hard work can be preserved on CD.

You no longer just conduct the repertoire of the most recent contemporary music, as you did at the outset, but the entire repertoire of the twentieth century. Your attitude as a conductor has also considerably changed from the early days of your career. How do you see this development today?

If I wished to summarize why I have conducted the music of the twentieth century and that of my own time, I would say that it was to submit myself to a demanding professional discipline. I told myself that if the concerts were hastily rehearsed and badly played, as was often the case with the music of the Second Viennese School immediately after the war, it was to the grave detriment of the music. I devoted myself to conducting works with what I would call an uncompromising discipline. I wanted the music of our time to be played with the same guarantee of professionalism and quality as is demanded of those musicians who play what is called the repertoire. Without that, there can only be wretched caricature.

Index of names

Donatoni, Franco (1927–2000) Italian composer 80, 132
Durieux, Frédéric (b. 1959) French composer 80

Eötvös, Peter (b. 1944) Hungarian conductor and composer 132

Furtwängler, Wilhelm (1886–1954) German conductor and composer 12, 59

Gielen, Michael (b. 1927) German conductor and composer 9, 10
Giugno, Peppino di (b. ??) Italian computer specialist 84, 85, 86
Glock, William (1908–2000) English music administrator, former Director of
   BBC Radio 3 and the Proms 6, 21, 22
Gluck, Christoph Willibald von (1714–87) German composer 40, 121
Guy, Michel French Minister of Culture in the 1970s 71, 81

Hanslick, Eduard (1825–1904) Viennese music critic 38
Hartmann, Karl-Amadeus (1905–63) German composer 17
Haydn, Franz Joseph (1732–1809) Austrian composer 6, 22, 26, 39, 77
Heisenberg, Werner (1901–76) German physicist 83, 90
Hindemith, Paul (1895–1963) German composer 5, 14, 32
Hurel, Philippe (b. 1955) French composer 80

Ives, Charles (1874–1954) American composer 27

Jansen, Jacques (1913–2002) French baritone 8
Joachim, Irène (1913–2001) French soprano 8

Kagel, Mauricio (b. 1931) Argentinian-born composer, performer and film-
   maker 80
Karajan, Herbert von (1908–89) Austrian conductor 100
Klemperer, Otto (1885–1973) German-born conductor and composer 12, 14–15
Kletzki, Paul (1900–73) Polish-born Swiss conductor 11
Knappertsbusch, Hans (1888–1965) German conductor 17
Kurtág, György (b. 1926) Hungarian composer 80

Levi, Hermann (1839–1900) German conductor 19
Ligeti, György (b. 1923) Hungarian composer 26, 27, 80
Liszt, Ferencz (1811–86) Hungarian composer, conductor and pianist 26,
   41–2, 60, 121
Long, Marguerite (1874–1966) French pianist 60

Maderna, Bruno (1920–73) Italian composer, conductor and teacher 4, 9, 10, 80
Mahler, Gustav (1860–1911) Austrian composer, conductor and pianist 11,
   14, 44–5, 47, 48, 49, 50, 51, 54, 55, 57, 120, 129, 132
Manoury, Philippe (b. 1952) French composer 80, 90, 93
Marger, Brigitte Director, Cité de la Musique 81
Masson, André (1896–1987) French painter, originally a Surrealist 7
Matthews, Max (b. 1926) American computer musician 86
Mendelssohn, Felix (1809–47) German composer, pianist, organist and con-
   ductor 26, 38, 42, 49

Mercure, Pierre (1927–66) French-Canadian composer and conductor 63
Messiaen, Olivier (1908–92) French composer, organist and teacher 11, 58, 63, 80, 129, 134, 135, 137, 138
Milhaud, Darius (1892–1974) French composer and pianist 8
Mitropoulos, Dimitri (1896–1960) Greek-born American conductor, composer and pianist 7
Mozart, Wolfgang Amadeus (1756–91) Austrian composer, keyboard-player, violinist, violist and conductor 26, 27, 32, 39, 40, 48, 53, 133
Munch, Charles (1891–1968) Franco-German conductor and violinist (born in Alsace) 48, 59
Mussorgsky, Modest (1839–81) Russian composer 32, 56

Nietzsche, Friedrich (1844–1900) German philosopher and critic 15, 52
Nono, Luigi (1924–1990) Italian composer 3, 80

Pehlivanian, George (b. 1964) American conductor 129
Petrassi, Goffredo (1904–2003) Italian composer, organist and teacher 80
Planck, Max (1858–1947) German physicist 82
Pompidou, Georges (1911–74) French statesman 82, 83
Pousseur, Henri (b. 1929) Belgian composer, teacher and theorist 3, 4, 5, 80
Prokofiev, Sergei (1891–1953) Russian composer and pianist 32

Ravel, Maurice (1875–1937) French composer and pianist 27, 30, 51, 56, 57, 58, 60, 61, 120, 137
Reich, Steve (b. 1936) American composer 80
Renaud, Madeleine (1900–94) French actress 3
Rihm, Wolfgang (b. 1952) German composer 80
Rimsky-Korsakov, Nikolai (1844–1908) Russian composer 62, 138
Robertson, David (b. 1958) American-born conductor, Director of Ensemble InterContemporain 1992–2000 80, 132
Rosbaud, Hans (1895–1962) Austrian conductor 3–6, 10, 63, 116n
Rousseau, Jean-Jacques (1712–78) Swiss philosopher, composer and writer on music 135

Sacher, Paul (1906–99) Swiss philanthropist and conductor 52–3
Sade, Marquis de (1740–1814) French writer 46
Scherchen, Hermann (1891–1966) German conductor 3
Schoenberg, Arnold (1874–1951) Austrian-born composer, conductor and teacher 9, 14, 22, 26, 43, 54, 77, 127, 128, 129, 131–2, 134
Schubert, Franz (1797–1828) Austrian composer 22, 27, 65
Schumann, Robert (1810–56) German composer, pianist, conductor and critic 22, 41, 42, 47, 49
Scriabin, Alexander (1872–1915) Russian pianist and composer 62
Snowman, Nicholas (b. ? 1944) English music administrator, former Director of IRCAM and co-founder of London Sinfonietta 71, 72, 81
Stadlen, Peter (1910–96) Austrian-born English pianist and music critic 66
Stein, Peter (b. 1937) German theatre and opera director 9
Stockhausen, Karlheinz (b. 1928) German composer 3, 4, 40, 77, 80, 101, 107–8, 128

General Index